BETWEEN THE BEGINNING AND THE END

Between the Beginning and the End

A Radical Kingdom Vision

J. H. BAVINCK

Translated by
Bert Hielema

WILLIAM B. EERDMANS PUBLISHING COMPANY
GRAND RAPIDS, MICHIGAN / CAMBRIDGE, U.K.

First published in Dutch under the title
De Mensch en zijn Wereld by
Bosch en Keuning, 1946.

This English edition © 2014 Wm. B. Eerdmans Publishing Co.
All rights reserved

Published 2014 by
Wm. B. Eerdmans Publishing Co.
2140 Oak Industrial Drive N.E., Grand Rapids, Michigan 49505 /
P.O. Box 163, Cambridge CB3 9PU U.K.

Library of Congress Cataloging-in-Publication Data

Bavinck, J. H. (Johan Herman), 1895-1964.
   [Mensch en zijn wereld. English]
   Between the beginning and the end: a radical kingdom vision /
Johan Herman Bavinck; translated by Bert Hielema.
     pages   cm
   ISBN 978-0-8028-7130-5 (pbk.: alk. paper)
   1. Jesus Christ — Person and offices. 2. Kingdom of God.   I. Title.

BT205.B2513   2014
232 — dc23

                                        2014008823

www.eerdmans.com

I dedicate this book to the memory of my parents,
SIETSE HIELEMA *and* MARTJE DE HAAN,
contemporaries of Johan Herman Bavinck.

Upon my immigration to Canada in 1951, they gave me the original Dutch version of the book, *De Mensch en zijn Wereld*. After so many years, I can now see that this book, more than any other, has shaped my vision for life.

Contents

Preface	viii
A Tribute to Johan Herman Bavinck by a Former Student	ix
A Brief Biographical Sketch	x
1. The Eternal in History	1
2. The Language of the Old Testament Symbols	14
3. The Kingdom	27
4. Christ, the Central Focus of Scripture	40
5. Christ's Arrest	53
6. The High-Priestly Verdict	65
7. "I Don't Know the Man"	78
8. The Sentence of the Governor	88
9. The Death of Humanity	102
10. Born Again	118
11. The Road to Life	130

Preface

The Dutch version of this book has been in my possession for more than six decades. Judging by the different colors of ink I used to underline certain passages — from green to red to black — I must have read the book several times. I have no idea why I suddenly started to translate the book in its entirety: I believe that the Spirit moved me, and the time was ripe. Only when I was actually busy translating the book in its entirety did I grasp its full beauty and its value for today.

I believe that Dr. Johan Herman Bavinck started to write this book during World War II, when all universities were closed by order of the German occupiers, and all students were either in hiding or were forced to work in Germany. It was published in 1946, when nuclear war posed an ever-greater threat to the world. That, I believe, accounts for the eschatological vision so prevalent in his writing, now even more relevant when climate change, resource depletion, and financial turmoil pose the greatest threats the world has ever faced.

I was very fortunate that my longtime friend Harry Van Dyke was willing to edit the manuscript. A professor of history emeritus at Redeemer University College, Harry has done a lot of translating himself, making him well qualified. The reason that this book reads as smoothly as it does is mainly due to his editing. My son-in-law, Richard P. Budding, my computer expert, was kind enough to design the page layout and formatting of the manuscript.

I have used the Grail Version of the Bible for the Psalms and the New International Version for other Bible quotations, except where indicated otherwise.

BERT HIELEMA

A Tribute to Johan Herman Bavinck by a Former Student

Dr. J. H. Bavinck was a wonderful, inspiring professor with a broad range of interests. His lectures were profound — always intellectually stimulating and spiritually enriching. They left an unforgettable impression on his students. His impact is best measured by the great stream of students who pursued their doctoral studies under his guidance. He was a missionary who thought it important to confront the world of Eastern religious thought with the message of Christ. His inspiring example left a powerful impression. A Brazilian who was studying with Dr. Bavinck when the professor had already become extremely fatigued and worn out testified, "He doesn't have to say much; just to see him once in a while is for me a fount of inspiration." I can identify with that sentiment.

Bavinck was a unique man who spoke from the heart — and through his life and deeds. It is no wonder that, shortly after he began to teach at the Free University of Amsterdam, he attracted many students from the United States and Canada. He was also a prolific and gifted author, one of those rare learned scholars who could write with childlike simplicity for less scholarly readers. All of his writings show his intimate and devotional knowledge of Scripture. He read the Bible as the book of daily encounters of God with humans. His fertile mind was always busy. From 1923 onward, there was scarcely a year without the publication of one or more books or articles. Many of them were devoted to missions; others were biblical studies and meditations.

JOHAN D. TANGELDER
October, 2000

A Brief Biographical Sketch

Johan Herman Bavinck was born on November 22, 1895, in Rotterdam, the Netherlands, where his father was a minister in the Gereformeerde Kerk. A nephew of the distinguished Dutch theologian Herman Bavinck, he studied theology at the Free University of Amsterdam from 1913 to 1918, and he continued his studies at the German universities of Giessen and Erlangen. He earned a doctorate in philosophy at the latter school in 1919.

That same year he sailed to the Dutch East Indies (now Indonesia) as an assistant pastor in the Reformed Church in Medan, on the island of Sumatra. From there he moved to the island of Java, to the central city of Bandung, where he ministered from 1921 to 1926. He went back to the Netherlands for three years as a pastor in Heemstede (1926-1929), but then returned to Indonesia as a professor of missions at the Theological School of Djokjakarta, also located in central Java, where he taught from 1934 through 1939.

Just before World War II, Bavinck returned to the Netherlands as a teacher of missions, first at Kampen Theological University, and later at his alma mater, the Free University of Amsterdam, as a professor in the fields of homiletics, liturgy, and related subjects. He remained there from 1939 until his death from kidney cancer in 1964.

Bavinck published a great number of works in the fields of biblical studies, missions, theology, philosophy, and psychology. Several of his works have been translated and published by the Bavinck Institute (under the auspices of Calvin Theological Seminary). Bavinck's radical "kingdom" vision is the most pronounced feature of *Between the Beginning and the End*, and this makes the book eminently suitable as a beacon directing us toward the new creation to come.

CHAPTER 1

The Eternal in History

The Concept of History

The people of the West have discovered history — perhaps their greatest discovery. With their far-seeing telescopes they have pulled the heavenly bodies so close that they have had to give up their secrets. And they have split the atom into its basic components. They have penetrated the mysterious forces that keep the universe together. All these discoveries have been magnificent, but the most important one of all is that the human race has discovered history. It is this that has changed its own existence and has given life on earth a new and glorious perspective.

This does not mean that the ancient peoples did not sense something of the miracle of history. They definitely understood that the individual is part of the whole and that everybody is part of some great happening from birth until death. They also carved certain dates into granite and elevated kings into figures of glory. They depicted battles and kept records of how nations rose and perished. All this they noted, but what escaped them was the dramatic course of global happenings. They did not have a comprehensive view of history: that is, they did not perceive that all those battles, the mighty deeds of their kings, the rise and fall of nations, were mere footnotes in the momentous process of the life of humanity, a process that continues from generation to generation and from century to century. They did not bother themselves with the question of whether all these events made sense, whether anything was accomplished, whether there was anything substantial that was worthy of being carried forward.

The ancient Indians saw history as a rushing stream from one period to the next, until everything would disappear into emptiness, the cycle would repeat itself, and new worlds would emerge in which identical happenings would again occur. To them, history was a mad race, dragging everything with it in a senseless *danse macabre,* repeating the cycle time and again from here to eternity.

But that misses the essence of history. We today have realized that history must be more than deadly repetition. We have examined the question of why things unfold as they do, and we have tried to view global happenings in one all-encompassing perspective. We have detected something of the drama of all this and have wondered what laws they obey and what thoughts they embody. And because we started to gain such a perspective, we have viewed the life of a single human being in a different context than that of those who preceded him.

After all, once we have experienced history, our own existence on earth is elevated to a new dimension. The people of old understood that individual lives run in similar pathways. In general, humans sail through their early years as in a dream: one moment elated and the next overcome with grief, sometimes moved by love and at other times consumed by hate. Later we are caught up in a never-ending struggle for life, moved to tears of joy when for the first time we hold our own child in our arms, the child we will later coach carefully through the pitfalls of life. Then we become older and weaker, our eyes grow dim and our feet move more slowly, till death calls us home. That is the course of life for all of us, and that pattern depicts the essence of the existence of the untold millions, those now living and those who went before us. All of our lives display a similar path. We may differ in strength and ability, and we may go our separate ways in education and development; yet, despite all these dissimilarities, there is the universal human condition that is always the same, the reason why we forever belong to each other.

In all this I am still looking at human beings apart from history. We see them in their individual existence from cradle to grave. It's a different matter, however, when we pay attention to them as part of history. Then we can picture them at a certain point in a dramatic process, where they experience the reality of their age and wrestle with the tensions so typical of their era. Then they help solve the problems of the age, or make them even more complicated, even more difficult to solve.

In short, when we regard modern humans this way, we see them in their historic setting, as a sudden flash of lightning between past and future. We then begin to realize that the lives of such people are transit points through which this grand process continues — that is, we can then see those humans as part of history. At first glance, we might see some similarity between a merchant in the Roman Empire and a CEO of a commercial enterprise in our time. They both deal with problems that accompany the encounter with the laws of economic reality, which are valid for all ages. But when we investigate the two lives a bit more closely, we discover that the comparison does not hold water. They stand at different points in time, and this determines their entire life. History has advanced during those two thousand years, which is why the human problems are also totally different. It is simply not possible to lift persons out of their time frame and milieu; we must regard them within the context of the totality of the particular period of history in which their lives were anchored. Only then do we see humans in their totality. After all, mankind is history. History is not an aspect of being human; it is at the very core of a person's life. This is the outlook that modern Western people have developed concerning history and the individual person's relationship to it.

Yet this discovery, however great and remarkable it may seem, is not nearly as exceptional as it may appear at first glance. After all, the Bible, too, has shown us history, and it, too, describes the human being as a creature who stands in history. The animal does not know history: it stands outside what's happening in its surroundings. Only we — men and women — have a place in history, and that place determines our life on earth.

In gripping visions, the prophets of old observed the dramatic course of world history, and they revealed for us something of God's dramatic plan that pervades all of history's phases. The Bible knows that we can never be regarded as "individuals" who are detached from all other realities, but rather that we are always, when seen in the right perspective, to be regarded within the totality of human history. That is where we stand, and it is what determines us: we are caught up in the web of history, and this connection rules our lives. Yes, we are part of God's plan for the world, a plan that rushes all the way from Adam to that overwhelming finish when the reign of the Antichrist will be destroyed by the coming again of the Son of man. Long before Hegel wrote about the philosophy of history, and Spengler ventured to postulate the decline of the West, the Bible, in a few dramatic lines, showed the grand perspective that permeates all of world history.

Based on what the Bible says about these happenings, Aurelius Augustine, that great thinker of antiquity, opened up for us a new perspective regarding God's plan for the human race in his book *The City of God*. Étienne Gilson, in his *Introduction à l'étude de Saint Augustine*, says: "Perhaps it was then for the first time that a human mind ventured to search for a synthesis of world history, thanks to the light of revelation which revealed to him its origin and hidden end." Augustine sensed the tragedy of what happens on our planet, but he also detected that all these happenings are not chaotic and senseless, but that God has a wise and holy meaning for all those goings-on. Augustine realized that, even in an era when the Roman Empire teetered on the brink of collapse, the essence of human existence is that we stand in history and that this history is the revelation of God's great plan. In his book *Augustinus*, Oepke Noordmans says of *The City of God*: "The pounding of the world's history rumbles through the book from start to finish."

This same Augustine also understood that our lives do not find their ultimate meaning in history. We are not mere creatures caught in the tempest of world events; we are not just thin strands along which the spark of global history is conducted from century to century. No, every living person also stands in a direct relationship to eternity. We have merit of our own, and God values our lives in themselves. Every human being, whoever he or she is, and wherever he or she is on the time line of history — all live in a constant relationship to God and can only be understood in terms of that relationship. Augustine, who expressed such lofty thoughts about the design of world history in his book *City of God*, says in one of his other writings: "I desire to understand God and my soul." He understood that we stand before God's face; that in the turbulent currents of the times we have to deal directly with God himself; and that eternity is an integral part of our existence. Augustine learned that from the Bible, and he lived his life fully conscious of that insight.

I would like to reflect on how the Bible sees us as human beings, seeking to understand how the Bible views us and what the Bible tells us about ourselves. One thing has already become clear: the Bible regards us both as being in history and standing before the face of God.

The Eternal in History

The Primitive Understanding of the Past

Before I elaborate a bit more thoroughly on the matters mentioned above, it would be helpful to focus for a moment on what the ideas of the so-called primitive peoples were concerning the origin and development of the universe. Their ideas coincide in the main with what we deem important today. One of the significant aspects concerning the thinking of some of the tribes in Asia and Africa is that they believe in an *Urzeit*, primordial time, the primeval period that preceded the time when humanity began life on earth. *Urzeit* was the time when all things were put in place. What happened, then, became the measure for everything that would happen afterwards. In that era the basis was laid on which all subsequent events rest. The concept of *Urzeit* appears in various forms. It is the time when the myths took place, those stories that play such an important role in the religious life of these tribal peoples. During that period, according to the Hindus, the world came into being through the sacrifice of a thousand-headed, thousand-footed giant, out of which arose sun and moon, heaven and earth, animals and plants. The different castes also originate from this giant. In other words, behind the existence of this well-ordered world appears a sacrifice in the *Urzeit*. Every sacrifice, even one offered by a priest in our time, is a repetition of what took place in prehistoric times. Everything that happened in the *Urzeit* predetermines what exists in our present world and what has taken place earlier. In the primeval time, according to the Aztecs of North America, the mother deity became pregnant. Her daughter, the moon goddess, and the four hundred stars ridiculed their mother and wanted to kill her. However, the child in her womb consoled and encouraged her, and when the moon goddess and the stars kept on pushing their mother to abort the child, the radiant sun god was born. With one blow he cut off the head of the moon goddess and expelled all four hundred star gods. All this happened in the *Urzeit*, but even now every year, when the days shorten and darkness prevails, the moon and the stars boast of their preeminence for a while, until, with the summer solstice, the sun again reappears in full force. Whatever happened in the time before history explains what now takes place every year.

When we strip these ideas of what, to our way of thinking, sounds rather childish, we are left with the core idea that the time in which we stand, the time in which history takes place, can never be understood in terms of itself. If we want to understand that — if we want to grasp the sense of history — we must go back to primeval times, to the events that took place before the ordering of this world. It was precisely then that the foundations were laid on which the structure of history rests.

It is truly remarkable that this same primitive thinking that is always engaged with the happenings in the *Urzeit* is at the same time interested in what will happen in the end-time. The gods and the powers at work in primeval times fashioned our world as we now experience it. However, the existence of this world is no more than a brief flash between two abysses of deep darkness. Soon, at the arrival of the end-time, our world will descend to the state it was in before, and everything will revert back to what existed in the *Urzeit*. Just as death is close to birth, so the downturn is not far from the upswing. Just as all that has been neatly ordered stems from chaotic disorder, emanating from the fog of the *Urzeit*, so the cosmos will disappear again in that same undefined state. The end-time is nothing else but the return to the *Urzeit*.

There truly is something very appealing in all this. Why does the sun come up every morning? It is because in the *Urzeit* some god caused its birth from the mother-womb of the East, and so the same thing happened and happens every morning from then on. Why does this particular mountain have such a bizarre shape? It is because in prehistoric times that same mountain took its shape as we now see it. Why does this particular river originate from that high mountaintop? Because in primeval time the gods or giants hit the mountains so hard with their powerful fists that water burst forth. Why is it that Hindu society has four castes? Because in the *Urzeit* four castes were born out of the giant who was sacrificed by the gods: the Brahmin caste came from his head, and the other castes from his arms, shins, and feet. Nothing in the world is there by chance; everything is there because it must be that way since it originated in that form in the *Urzeit*. And beyond the horizon lies the end-time, in which all cosmic reality shrinks away into the mistiness of the one Being that existed before all things came to be. History is a small strip of land between the two oceans of *Urzeit* and end-time. Our being in the world is but a short moment: behind us we have the horizon of primeval time and before us the horizon of the end-time, and these two are one and the same.

The Eternal in History

The vision offered by these old myths is not without merit for us. That we exist as we do can only be explained from the events that occurred in the period preceding our time. If we are to understand the hidden mainsprings of our lives, we must not look at ourselves in our existence here and now, but we must go back to what happened in prehistory. All of history is preceded by the mystery of the *Urzeit*, which gives meaning to the here and now.

The Bible, however, gives an entirely different perspective from that presented in the ancient myths. Yet the Bible does speak of an *Urzeit*, a period prior to the age in which we live. In the biblical *Urzeit* — if that is the correct term in this case — the visible things were born, and God ordered this wonderful creation. Then God made a place for the sun and moon; he arranged for day to succeed the night; he separated water from land; and he assigned to each creature the task that it was to fulfill in the harmonious context of God's world. However, the Bible places the Fall into sin in that same *Urzeit*. During that time we fell away from God and rose up against him. The Fall into sin is a historic event: it happened in history. But it is, on the other hand, also suprahistorical because it had consequences for all subsequent centuries. All of human history can only be understood in terms of this one event. Whatever else happens with us and whatever else we do, all of it is fundamentally tied in with this awesome reality that we humans are God's creatures and that we fell into sin. In other words, our total existence can only be understood from the point of view of the *Urzeit*. The entire course of human history remains a closed book for those who fail to recognize what in essence is the basis of it all.

Just as the Bible, in a few sober words, depicts the *Urzeit* that foreshadows world history, so it outlines for us the end-time as well, the confluence of everything. The history of the world ends in God's judgment. When we look at the very last pages of the book of Revelation, we cannot fail to notice how similar these chapters are to the first sections of the book of Genesis. Again we read about the Tree of Life; again we see the description of the river of the water of life; again we are confronted with the terrifying aspects of the divine judgment. The end-time again picks up the threads that have determined human life throughout the ages: in the end-time all things return to their beginning. Just as the book of Genesis paints paradise for us, the place where human life started, so the

Revelation of John brings us back to that same place. End-time and *Urzeit* are intimately related. In short, the end-time reveals again the realities of the *Urzeit*.

And we, the human race, are positioned between these two — between *Urzeit* and end-time. This is where history finds its place. History is thus not an event without boundaries; it is not something that arises out of the haze of an unknown past that will someday end up in an undetermined future. No, history is delineated territory: from its very inception it is anchored in its basic form. History is the spark that jumps from the *Urzeit* to the end-time, from the first paradise to the final one in which God himself will be both light and temple. History can do nothing else but stir up, again and again, the awesome forces that were born in the *Urzeit*. History can only realize what was revealed in the primeval era: the terrible, fatal, ruinous renunciation of God, and in contrast to that the magnificent reality of God's grace. The entire mighty drama of life involving all nations and races — all the wars and calamities, all the hate and misery, all failures and pains — all this is nothing but the direct consequence of "the tragedy of tragedies" that took place in the *Urzeit*.

And when all these centuries, with their troubles and tears, are history, then the thread will be picked up again at the coming of the divine judgment that the world will face. To stand in history means to stand in the flash between those two, between the beginning and the end. To be human means to have a place between those two, between *Urzeit* and end-time, between the two trees in the beginning and the judgment in the end.

That is how the Bible depicts, in living color, the life of us men and women, each with his or her own life to live, each directly related to eternity, and each simultaneously caught up in history.

Enduring Realities

There are indeed enduring realities that dominate human life. We are able to love and hate, to wage war and conclude peace, to be deep thinkers who constantly probe the secrets of life or to be people who are natural leaders, always the first to take the bull by the horns. As citizens of the earth we can use our talents in manifold ways, but the possibilities are limited.

We can never distance ourselves from who we are, never go beyond the deepest realities that determine our being. We have only limited space in which to maneuver because all our actions are fenced in by our inability to be different from who we are.

The Bible speaks to us about these enduring realities in several places. The Bible repeatedly pushes through the random and temporal and penetrates to the underlying foundation that is unaffected by the course of time. Precisely because it does this and never limits itself to what is accidental, or current, or incidental, the Bible is a book that is never outdated. Pharaoh's empire is long gone; there is no longer any trace of all those small nations, of the Philistines, the Moabites, the Ammonites, or the Edomites; gathered to their fathers millennia ago are Potiphar, Ahab, Naaman, and the rich young ruler. However, what the Bible portrays for us in their lives has never changed. The Bible has been translated into the languages of most nations, and it has been transported through the centuries. Why? Because it is always and everywhere current and real, and it deeply influences the thinking of all people.

There is something in human life that is historically determined, that is characteristic of a certain time and cannot easily be understood and appreciated in other times. But there is also something in human nature that is not subject to change and is valid in all circumstances. The latter typifies the Bible.

In the Bible we repeatedly encounter the concept of "the human being." The term does not denote this or that person, but the human being in his or her essential stature, the way he or she exists. Some words in the Bible express this specifically: for instance, the Old Testament uses the word *adam* to indicate the human race in its entirety — humanity as such. Genesis 6:3 tells us that the Spirit of the Lord will not be at odds with the human race forever. We meet it again in Job 5:7, where we read that "the human being is born to trouble as surely as sparks fly upward." The ears of the believing Israelite attuned to the Old Testament heard in the word *adam* a variety of sounds that for us no longer resonate in the word "human," at least not to that extent. The word *adam* reminded an Israelite immediately of the first Adam, whom God formed from the dust of the earth. That made the word eminently suitable to typify the human race in its unbreakable unity. The Israelite sensed something of the fact that humans are earthbound. A human being, *adam*, belongs to *adamah*, the life-bearing earth. With every sinew of his existence, he is tied to the earth, which bears him and feeds him. This is the reason why there are strains of transitoriness and perishability in the word *adam*, of vulnerability and insignificance.

The whole concept of "humanity" is really remarkable. It does not mean the sum of all people who have ever lived and will live. Neither is it a poetic personification; it is 100 percent real. There is indeed something like that mysterious entity "humanity" that is present in every human being. Behind all individual characteristics, behind all differences of race and language, there lies "humanity," which through all ages is and remains the same.

It has been said that the reason the great poets in history — the unforgettable writings of the Greek poets of tragedy, of Dante and Shakespeare, Goethe and Ibsen — continue to be read is that they do not depict a particular person but in their works penetrate to the mystery of the human being as such, the person with his or her burning desires and never-ending longings, the human being in his or her smallness and nobility. If that is true, then we can declare that the Bible is the greatest of all poems. It is the song of "the human," of the *adam* born of the earth. When we read the Bible, we are never imprisoned in historical trivia, but we hear the universally human beyond the individual particulars, and we detect in their situation and life our own story.

This fact is of such importance that it will continue to occupy our attention in what follows in this study. Many words in the New Testament can only be understood when we have totally assimilated the concept of "the human being" as it forms the basis of all proclamation of the gospel in the Bible. When Paul deals with putting on the clothing of "the new humanity" and discarding "the former humanity," he is dealing with realities that remain hidden for all those who have not understood the biblical concept of "the human being."

The ancient church fathers often focused their attention on this biblical way of speaking. They pointed out that the lost sheep in the parable by that name is not a certain individual, but "the human being" in its lost state. The fathers dealt repeatedly with "human nature" and "the human race," and they were witnesses to the fact that, where Christ is the groom, the bride is none other than "the human." The old legend that Adam was buried on Golgotha's hill and was baptized there by the blood and water dripping from Jesus' side was plainly inspired by the desire to show that "the human" as such was baptized and saved through Jesus Christ. These same church fathers dealt with Adam often and eagerly, and each time it is apparent that by Adam they mean the human being as such, the eternal Adam.

When we wonder what is really at the biblical core of the concept "human," several ideas come to the fore. Earlier we associated the word *adam* with its close affinity to the earth: we are *adam*, that is to say, we are fragile, perishable, bound to the dust out of which we have been fashioned. That same hint of brittleness and mortality we also find in other words used in the Bible for the human race: "What are mortals that you are mindful of them?" (Ps. 8:5). It is expressed especially strongly in addressing us as "flesh," the title so often assigned to us humans: "All flesh is like grass and all his glory is like flowers of the field. The grass withers and the flowers fall because the breath of the Lord blows on them" (Isa. 40:6-7). In that designation of "flesh," there is always something of the divine smile concerning our self-conceit that makes us believe we are able to accomplish great things: "Dust you are and to dust you shall return" (Gen. 3:19). The apostle Paul, in his letter to the Corinthians, muses about the deeper meaning of the Adam name and positions the earthbound *adam* over against "the last Adam, who has become a life-giving spirit" (1 Cor. 15:45).

Yet it would be unjust and one-sided if we were to place too much emphasis on the fragility and mortality that is so much part of the word *adam*. After all, that same notion of Adam contains very different elements, pointing to other realities. To be Adam also includes being created in the image of God, who called the heavens and the earth into being. To be Adam also means to be lord of creation, means to be a lowercase "god," to whom all things are subject. We, as image-bearers of God, are not only *adam*, earthbound, but are also rulers who have been called to do great works. We will probably never fully understand what exactly is meant by those wonderful words of Genesis 1:27 — that we have been created "in the image of God." But one thing is clear: we can do some real probing of God's deepest thoughts that he incorporated in creation. Only we humans, the *adam* of all creatures, are capable of uncovering the hidden powers of the world and making them subject to us, we who have become "living souls" because the Lord God breathed the *adam* of life into our nostrils. After all, we are Adam: we are that unique thinking part of the universe that knows what it is, that has the capacity of self-knowledge. We are that Adam in whom the universe comes to self-consciousness, having the capacity to praise our maker. We are Adam, God's children (Luke 3:38). We will always retain some of that high rank and noble status, even though sin has disfigured and corrupted us, even though all sorts of features in our being are completely perverted and distorted. We remain image-bearers. We can never degenerate into being an animal: we will always retain something in us that makes us different. We will always retain the shreds of the broken halo, thanks to the inalienable in us, the last vestiges of God's image. Henceforth we are indeed able to live the lie, to lose our way in our own foolish fantasies, to fancy a world completely different from the world God has created, to give ourselves over to vain and sinful deliberations. But we cannot not think, we cannot revert to being an animal, even though we might wish to do so. Even though every creation of our brain can be turned against God, and even though we can resist God's will with all our might and use all our faculties to shield ourselves against God's judgments, still we cannot not create. We simply must always think and create, always act, always care. That is because we are human, we are *adam*. God's image, which once adorned us, can be distorted, can become unrecognizable, can be made into a caricature; yet it can never totally disappear. God's image is so deeply etched into our being that no human hands, however abusive, can ever erase its features.

However, in the word *adam* there is yet another element, the element of the curse. A massive and somber curse is suspended over the life of humanity. That curse fell on us when we, in our disobedience, turned away from God and chose to go our own way in the world, even though that curse would remain with us throughout the ages. To be human now also means to be bearer of that curse, a curse that rests on all human endeavor as an immense burden. In the hands of us humans, all achievements in the technical field and all progress in knowledge and practical matters can lead to horrible outcomes. The curse is evident in social life, reveals itself in international affairs, and stifles any attempt to better the life of others. That the curse exists is no secret; yet its presence remains a mystery. That's why we are at times suddenly shocked by what we are doing, scared to continue on with it. That's why the people of the Western world look to the future with anxiety. We humans, in a surge of bravado and tenacity, may accomplish great feats, but sooner or later we always encounter that tenacious element of fatal powerlessness that prevents us from establishing a lasting peace. We can never overcome the curse that keeps us from achieving shalom.

Thus the simple word *adam* is loaded with content and chock-full of ideas. No matter how talented and capable we are in our daily lives, we are defined and limited by what is contained in the term *adam*. We can never free ourselves from the limitations that are posed by that word; we can never be or become something different from what this name signifies from its very inception. That is why there is something monotonous in history, in spite of all its variations. World history is the record of that single person, of *adam* in all his or her wanderings and experiences, in all his or her struggles and hopes, in all victories and defeats, in creativity and thinking — it is the life story of *adam* in exile.

CHAPTER 2

The Language of the Old Testament Symbols

The Temple

We humans stand in history with both our feet planted on the earth. That makes us different from any other species, either animals or plants, who are indeed alive but whose existence is not tied in with history because their lives are basically determined by biology. From age to age they use their biological function according to identical natural laws, but in all this they do not make history. History comes to the fore only where we encounter spiritual and moral forces, where progress and growth are found. That's why we speak of history only in terms of the human race.

That does not mean that human life is exhausted in history. There are two facets of us that operate outside history. The first is the biological one, that of breathing, eating, drinking, and all the other bodily functions. These functions do not fit within the realm of history; they are below the cutoff point for history. But we humans also have a touch of eternity in us, of something imperishable, something that transcends history. Still, we are *adam* and thus are intimately tied to firm, immovable elements. It is particularly that "eternal" something in us where religion enters the picture. The Bible speaks about *adam* and teaches us its redemption. In this chapter we will repeatedly encounter this aspect.

A casual glance at the Old Testament worship service reveals that its symbolism treats of human beings in their fallen state, living under a miserable curse and subjected to death and damnation. It reveals that temple worship is not a random collection of symbols and ceremonial acts but an organic whole that interprets the fundamental truths that determine human life in clear forms for all to see. That is why we should see these symbols in a wider context and thus take from these symbols what God has to say to *adam*.

We are first confronted by the Temple. We must look at that Temple as it was constructed at a certain time in the history of Israel, during the rule of Solomon, the son of David. Of course, we must not forget that, before the Temple was built as a place of worship, Israel already had the Tabernacle, which was made according to divine designs: "See that you make them according to the pattern shown you [Moses] on the mountain" (Exod. 25:40). In order to understand the meaning of worship, therefore, the Tabernacle is in some ways even more important than the later Temple of Solomon. On the other hand, we should not forget that in the Temple several ideas are better expressed than in the Tabernacle, which was constructed to be carried during Israel's wanderings in the desert. When the Temple was built, the architect had unlimited opportunity to show his talents, as he was not bound by the limitations inherent in a portable structure. We must also look at the Temple in the light of the prophecy of Ezekiel, who deals with divine worship in the last chapters of his book. Based on these givens, we will attempt to form an idea of the meaning of the Temple and what went on during the ceremonies on a daily basis.

Already in antiquity people thought that Israel's temple was a depiction of the world and its fullness. That view was expressed, for instance, by Philo, the learned Jewish writer, and later expressed by several of the early church fathers, such as Justin Martyr and Clement of Alexandria. Taken by itself, this view is not that strange; in fact, almost everywhere in the world sacred buildings, especially temples that various peoples have erected, express the views then held about the makeup of the universe. In the Far East the ancient understanding of the cosmos was that a high mountain was situated at the center of the world, and the gods dwelt on that mountain (*meru* in Hindi). On the various mountainsides were located the four parts of the world, surrounded by the infinite world ocean. Numerous holy places in the Far East plainly show this *meru* type, a mountain of the gods adorned with all the symbolic ornamental paraphernalia suitable for such a sacred mountain. We see this especially in Thailand, Vietnam, and Cambodia, and on several Indonesian islands, such as Bali. Even though the temple buildings in the Ancient Near East and in Egypt were of a different structure, there is sufficient evidence to assume that they, too, were meant to be symbolic expressions of the then current conception of the world. In other words, the temple is the world in a nutshell, a microcosm, with the deity living at its center.

Based on that, the idea that the Temple in Israel was also meant to be a depiction of the world is not out of place. In some respects this is also confirmed by Scripture itself, even though the Bible does not overemphasize these matters. The book of Hebrews intimates that "the sanctuary made with hands" (9:24) was a foreshadowing of heaven itself. And if the Holy of Holies represented *heaven* and made it real in the world, then it is logical to assume that the outer court around the Temple was a prototype of the *world*. Both the inner Temple and the outer court point back to the two hemispheres of heaven and earth and show in symbolic form the magnificent edifice that is God's great world.

There are several other places in Scripture that illuminate these matters even more. We should note, in the first place, that the temple's Holy of Holies, as well as the Holy Place, was decorated with images of palm trees and flowers. In 1 Kings 6:29 we are specifically told that Solomon had all the walls of God's house adorned with wooden sculptures of cherubim, palm trees, and open flowers. In other words, the inner Holy Place was completely portrayed as a garden of golden flowers. C. van Gelderen explains this section of the temple as follows: "Perhaps the palm trees represent the trees in paradise, guarded by the cherubim (Gen. 3:24). What is striking is that all the wall adornments — except for the cherubim — are replicas of flowers. My conclusion is that these represent the Garden of Eden, guarded by cherubs. It makes sense also on theological grounds to view the temple as a facsimile of paradise, to which free access can only be obtained by way of atonement, while honoring the highest regard for the Lord's holiness, which is ensured by the presence of the cherubs."

If this commentator is correct, we can see paradise both in the Holy Place and in the Holy of Holies itself. Paradise has not been relegated to bygone history but is still omnipresent and situated right among us, since it is placed by God at the center of the world, with the condition that paradise is now hidden behind heavy curtains, while cherubim guard the entrance. By means of these symbolic representations, what happened in paradise and what happened in the *Urzeit* have become a permanent reality.

The Language of the Old Testament Symbols

This interpretation brings us back to paradise. Even though Genesis 2 does not explicitly say so, everything indicates that paradise was situated on a high mountain. The land of Eden is the source of a great river, which in the garden becomes four great rivers, all of them flowing into the various countries of the world. Thus we can visualize paradise as situated on a high plateau containing the fountainheads of mighty rivers. We can leave aside what four rivers these are meant to represent. The main point is that these four rivers represent the streams that irrigate the major countries of the world — and hence provide the world with riches and life. Paradise, lying at the center of the world, is the source of the world's precious water. Paradise discloses the secret of the well-being and beauty of the world: it is particularly here that God reveals his presence.

It is evident from other places in the Bible that we must see paradise as situated on a mountain or a mountain range. For instance, Ezekiel 28:13-14 says of Tyre that it was located in Eden, the garden of God, on the holy mount of God. Much in these words is not quite clear, but they do indicate that the prophet Ezekiel imagined paradise as situated on a mountain. This is confirmed in Revelation 21:10, where the New Jerusalem, the new paradise, is also shown as situated on a "great and high mountain."

Thus paradise lies in a mountainous region, in the heart of the world, from whence the world receives its life. Once we have seen this, we are not surprised that the Temple, too, was built on a mountain — Mount Zion. Even though this mountain was very small, almost insignificant, it was chosen by God as the mountain where he would reveal his presence. That is the reason Psalm 68:6 exclaims with exuberance: "Why gaze in envy, O rugged mountains, at the mountain where God has chosen to live?" And the prophet Isaiah views it as a powerful sign of the end-time when he writes: "In the last days the mountain of the Lord's temple will be established as chief among the mountains" (2:2). The Temple is, therefore, the everlasting paradise that is situated on a mountain in the heart of the world.

The majestic vision that Ezekiel sees in chapter 47 fits into that pattern as well. In that vision he sees a stream flowing from the temple, and he notices that it flows to the south. That rivulet, originating from the sanctuary, grows wider and carves out a broad stream that brings life and prosperity wherever it flows. This river of life, with paradise as its source, is the fount of blessings for the world. The pool of Siloam, originating from the foot of the Temple Mount — hence flowing, as it were, from the Temple itself — has a similar meaning (cf. Isa. 8:6; John 9:7).

I should point out that the entrance of the Temple faces east, where the sun rises, and thus points to the origin of life. Whoever enters the Temple turns his back to the east and proceeds to the west, the country where the sun sets, the region of death. Among many peoples, houses face west so that those who enter turn toward life and the light. In many countries only the reigning monarch may build his palace facing east, because he who enters there surrenders to a life-or-death verdict. This is also true of the Temple: whoever enters the holiness of God faces death. Only through death can we appear before God's face; going to God means meeting with death. And yet that same God is the source of life, indeed, the source of all life in the world.

In summary, we have come to the conclusion that the Holy of Holies represents a replica of paradise, which in the *Urzeit* was the domicile of humanity; that paradise is protected by cherubim, the guardians of God's holiness; and that paradise is still the fountain of all strength and vitality, and is situated at the center of the world as an imperishable reality. In that paradise we once dwelt, but we have been banished from it. As exiles we have been thrown into the hard and troublesome world, but what once transpired in paradise still determines our entire history. We can never free ourselves from the consequences of what took place there.

The Priest

Only one man, the high priest, was allowed to enter the Holy of Holies, and then only once a year. Who is this person who is permitted to do what "Adam" could not do, that is, to return to paradise? Who is he who can bypass the flaming swords of the cherubim and again approach the Tree of Life and even come before the face of God himself?

In itself, the word "priest" (*cohen* in Hebrew) teaches us little about his essential function. The word stems from a verb that means "to stand" and has no other meaning than "he who stands." That is, the priest stands before the face of God; he is in God's service. The oldest annals do not mention priests as a separate class. Abraham personally does the ceremony for himself and his family, and the same applies to the other patriarchs. The head of the family or extended family is simultaneously the priest for his clan.

At a later stage of Israel's development, the office of priest became much more regulated. As an important function it became the special domain of a certain sector of the population. The priest occupied a special place in the center of the nation. He gave lessons in religion; he was entrusted with judging all kinds of difficult cases; and in extreme situations he was enabled — by means of the Urim and Thummim, which he carried in his breastplate — to determine the way shown by God. He also needed to ensure the ritual purity of the people, for example, to decide in cases of leprosy or other diseases whether the afflicted person must be regarded as either clean or unclean. But his most important duty was his service in the sanctuary. According to the memorable expression in the Epistle to the Hebrews, he was "selected from among men" and "appointed to represent them in matters related to God, and to offer gifts and sacrifices for sins" (Heb. 5:1). In other words, the priest pleaded for the people: he represented the people before God.

We should note that in the Old Testament the people of Israel were specifically chosen by God to be separate from other nations. This separation was not definitive and did not have an absolute character, but from its inception it was meant to underscore the fact that through Abraham's seed "all peoples and nations should be blessed." That was why the people of Israel could be called "a priestly nation" (Exod. 19:6). Just as the priest represented the people over against God, so did Israel in its entirety represent the world before God's face. This representation tied in with the covenant bond by which God bound himself to Israel and, in Israel, to all of humanity. The covenant idea is one of the most significant features of the Hebrew religion. Other nations have expressed themselves with a totally different attitude toward their gods and their religious world. Among many of them, the connection between gods and people is one of relationship, of descent. Their thinking was that the people are of divine origin and, owing to that common root, partake of divine powers. Others conceive of the relationship between God and the human world as one of the part to the whole. Humans are a small spark originating from the great fire of the deity, a drop from the ocean of God. We could label these two notions of the relationship between God and us as the *genealogical* and the *totalitarian* relationship. However, in contrast to the above religions, we find in Israel the federative, or *covenant,* association, characterized by the unique phenomenon that we cannot claim a single right vis-à-vis God, but that God has unilaterally, out of sovereign grace, bound himself to us and given us his promise. This same covenant structure is now of decisive importance for our entire fellowship with God.

This covenant has, of course, two aspects. In the first place, it is of a theological nature: we and God have a covenant relationship. Second, this covenant also contains a social element: God deals with us as humanity by means of the one man who is the mediator and who represents us all before God. That one person does not stand there as an individual, as a human being with all kinds of special qualities and talents; rather, he stands before God as the *adam,* as the person who bears the curse and has been banished from paradise. In short, he stands there as bearer of the imperishable in us, of the suprahistorical. Centuries may pass, wars may bring misery and devastation on the nations, but the priest as the mediator between God and us stands above history, representing that which does not change. We can also say it differently: the priest is Adam. In the figure of the priest, Adam again enters paradise, approaches the cherubim, and positions himself before the throne of the Almighty. That is the ultimate meaning of the annual ritual in which the high priest enters the Holy of Holies. He leaves behind the hit-or-miss historical situation in which he lives, loses fixation with day-to-day affairs that anchor him in history, rises far above history by descending back into the *Urzeit,* and enters paradise. That is the human's strand of the eternal, woven through the ups and downs of history.

These different features are even more visible when we pay attention to some other particulars that the Bible reveals about the office of priest. In the first place, note the sash worn by the high priest, described in Exodus 39:29. This sash was woven of fine linen with blue, purple, and scarlet yarn. The same colors adorned the high priest's breastplate (Exod. 28:15) and were also found in other places of his white garment. We are not nearly familiar enough with the ancient symbolism of these colors to understand what they mean. Philo — and later Flavius Josephus — were of the opinion that these four colors represented the several elements that together form the world. In this scheme, white would be seen as the earth, purple as water, the deep blue as the heavens, and the scarlet as fire. The four colors of the high priest's garment would together represent the cosmos and thus depict the high priest as born of the earth and belonging to that earth (see Hastings' *Dictionary of the Bible.*) However, this explanation is most likely incorrect, because the classification of the four elements is never found in Israel, even though it is quite common in Greece and the Far East. In numerous nations of antiquity, the four principal colors were intimately linked to the points of the compass: white is associated with the west, red with the east, black with the north, while the color of the south can vary. Nor is that kind of symbolism foreign to the Old Testament. For example, in Zechariah 6:1-8 we read of a vision in which horses appear with definite colors, going out to the four corners of the world: the white color in that passage points to the west, the red to the east, the black to the north, and the dappled color to the south. Of course, it is possible that the four colors of the high priest's garment point to the four quarters of the world; if so, they would together stand for the entire world as represented in the high priest.

But it is possible to understand the four colors in a different sense. Purple was the royal color in Israel, understood to be the image of royal dignity. This may be connected to the fact that, in the Far East and the Middle East, kings were thought to be associated with the direction of east: the royal palace as a rule would face the east, and the color purple, the color of the rising sun, would thus be associated with the eastern quarter of the world. About blue we know very little. Numbers 15:38-39 seems to suggest that there is a certain connection between the color blue and the law of the Lord, but how that connection was conceived is uncertain. We know for certain that the color white portrays purity, an aspect that has such a prominent place in the worship service. Just what "purity" meant for the average Israelite is not easy for us to imagine, because it was associated with numerous notions that lie outside our way of thinking. In many nations the color white is closely associated with the concept of death, sunset, and thus the west. We do not know whether — or to what extent — these associations were reflected in Israel. About the color scarlet we can say very little.

In all, very little is known for certain about these colors. What is certain, however, is that they were not chosen because they were such nice colors. No doubt they symbolize all kinds of notions and ideas. For our purpose, however, the principal point is that these four colors adorning the high priest's garment were also found in the temple — and especially in the Holy Place. The curtain described for us in 2 Chronicles 3:14 consisted of identical material: blue, purple, and crimson yarn, and fine white linen. Whenever the high priest entered the Temple, he wore these same colors, which characterized the Temple itself. There he entered his own world; there, in that paradise that God had installed in the midst of this world, he belonged; there was his home, his land of origin. There his humanity was counted as belonging to paradise, as part and parcel of that Garden of Eden where God had assigned him a place. The gold that the high priest carried signified that he also belonged to God himself, that he was Adam, son of God.

The breastplate with the different precious gems on which were engraved the names of Israel's tribes refers to the unique place occupied by the high priest in relation to the people: he represents the nation and acts as advocate before the face of God. I will not go into further details about the high-priestly clothing. Suffice it to say that the high priest is none other than *adam*, humanity in its essential state.

This emerges most strikingly in the mysterious figure of Melchizedek, who for a brief moment steps into the story of Abraham's life (Gen. 14) and is later mentioned in Psalm 110 and the book of Hebrews, of which the seventh chapter is especially important for our purpose. There it says quite explicitly that Melchizedek was "without father, without mother, without genealogy, without beginning of days or end of life" (Heb. 7:3). He stands outside and above history, does not have a place in any genealogy, does not belong to a specific era, and is not a link between two generations. He has something in him of imperishable eternity: he is *adam*, humanity in the final spark of its paradise glory. To be elevated above history is the striking feature of the priestly office. The priest represents humanity in the imperishable principles of its existence, and the priest belongs to the *Urzeit*, to paradise, where the explanation of all the problems that dominate history is to be found. That the priest Melchizedek suddenly emerges from the mist of obscurity to rise up before us as the priest of the most high God is the reason why his priestly office is so real and of such an elevated importance. He personifies humanity, the image-bearer of God, the one who belongs in paradise. All the later prophets of Israel stand at the center of history: they are historical figures through and through, figures who arise at a certain moment of time in history and do their work. But the priest stands above history in the sphere of immutability.

When we observe these matters in their interconnections, it is clear that we need to see the priest as *adam*, as "humanity personified," as the wanderer along the borders of paradise who in the core of his essence belongs to that paradise and knows it to be the cradle of his being.

The Problem of the Priestly Office

The foregoing takes us at once to the problem of this office. How is it possible for the fallen and exiled creature to return to paradise? In what way can this person go past the flaming swords of the cherubim and enter again in the vicinity of the Tree of Life, which is growing up before the throne of the Almighty? How can he go into the Holy of Holies without being destroyed?

That problem lies at the heart of the entire Old Testament religion. The entire Old Testament is nothing but one detailed, explicit, and thoroughly researched answer to the most central question that the human race has ever asked itself. And when we attempt to read this answer, we encounter some very essential elements. The first thing that is striking is that everything in the Old Testament goes back to the covenant God made with us. We stand before God in a covenant relationship, and it is this connection that rules us totally. God, in his unspeakable grace, opened a way to his promise when all possible avenues were cut off. God's covenant promise is the only basis on which the relationship with God is founded.

Second, we must keep in mind that the high priest, *adam*, when he enters the Holy of Holies, always carries blood. The sacrifice has preceded his entrance, and he carries the blood of the sacrificial animal with him into the sanctuary. That sacrificial animal is obviously meant as a substitute: it is humanity itself that is being offered. Only through death can Adam bypass the cherubim; only in death can he approach God's throne. Adam, who once aimed to be God's equal, now walks with head bowed. He comes to God, fully recognizing his blood-guilt and humbly surrendering his heart, returning to the place from which he was banned. The entire ceremonial sacrifice service in the Old Testament is anchored in this reality.

Third, we must realize that the sacrifice that took place in the outer court of the temple could only represent humanity because, according to God's plan of salvation, the true Adam, the Lamb of God that takes away the sin of the world, would one day surrender himself to death to pay the world's debt. Thus does the problem of the priestly office find its solution in Christ, for only in Christ is this priestly office possible.

Finally, we must note that the cherubim in the Holy of Holies are not depicted as carrying a flaming sword, but are looking down at the cover of the ark. Here, in the Holy of Holies, they have put aside their terrible and frightening weapons and stand in worshipful admiration before the mystery that made possible what in its deepest essence is actually impossible: Adam can again approach God's throne (Exod. 25:20). This is what Peter means when he says that "even angels desire to look into those things" (1 Pet. 1:12). These cherubim gaze uninterruptedly at that cover as if they want to say: "We do not understand your miraculous works, O God of light and compassion, but we bow before your majesty."

The Holy Place

Paradise is not the normal habitat of the church. The church is indeed always present during her stay on earth, but she really lives at the edge of paradise, because paradise is not the place where she can permanently reside during this world period. Only once a year may the high priest enter there, promising that Adam, too, may once again approach the Tree of Life. The usual place where the church lives and breathes is the Holy Place. That portion of the Temple is a wonderful area. It is not yet the Holy of Holies, not yet the full glory of paradise; but it is also not the world, with its curse and misery — it lies between the two. Paradise is the place where God reveals himself, and it is surrounded by the world. In that Holy Place we encounter the church's normal life functions. It is here that the priest enters every morning; where the priest burns the fragrant incense; where the table with the bread of the Presence is situated; where the candlestick or lampstand spreads its light. Within the world system the church has her very own place, rooted in the Holy Place.

The different objects in the Holy Place relate, in figurative language, the life of the church in her many aspects. First and foremost are the two figures facing each other: the lampstand on the south side and the table holding the bread of the Presence on the north side. Hellmuth Frey, in his *Das Buch der Kirche in der Weltwende* ("The Book of the Church at the Turning Point in History"), sees in the lampstand the universal tree that, according to the stories of the Ancient Near East, portrayed the universe with its roots in Hades, its trunk bearing fruit rising up in this world, and at the top, the sun, moon, and the five planets. However, scripturally speaking, there is more reason to assume that this lampstand represents the church herself in her function as bearer of light in this dark world. "The seven lampstands are the seven churches," says John in his Revelation on Patmos (Rev. 1:20), and this idea is totally in agreement with what we have found elsewhere regarding this lampstand. The lampstand is the church, but a church seen in a very special form. The church carries the light that shines in the darkness. The light she carries is a gift, a gift that emanates from God himself. That precious present is wonderfully expressed in Zechariah's vision of the golden lampstand and the two olive trees "that serve the Lord of all the earth" (Zech. 4:1-14). The oil that the lights receive from the bowl at the top of the lampstand, as Zechariah sees it, comes directly from the olive trees, whose branches are bent over the lampstand. The light that the lampstand spreads is the light that originates directly from God: it reflects the glow that radiates from God's face.

The bread of the Presence (Exod. 25:30) is not further discussed in Scripture. What is clear is that bread in the Bible is always a sign of life and strength. We live by bread. These loaves are the symbols of the life of the church, the power she derives every day from these loaves. These loaves are God's gift, but they also function as a gift offering from the church to God. The church receives this gift and dedicates it to God. The church is in the world as a church of light and of life; both come from God, and both are also recommitted to God. The two aspects of the church, expressed by the lampstand and the bread of the presence, point to the essence of the church and indicate that her existence in the world is made up of both gift and offering.

Both these aspects culminate in the altar of incense situated on the west side of the Holy Place. There the light and life of the church are expressed in adoration. Adoration is the end result — the ultimate function — of the church. On that altar of incense are the live coals conceived as coming from God (Isa. 6:6), while the incense is the human contribution. The incense altar is the meeting point, the place where human thought and God's grace encounter each other and where every thought becomes adoration.

It is striking that in the Holy Place the fourth object is absent: on the east side there is nothing. The lampstand has its counterpart in the table of the bread of the presence, but the incense altar has no match in the Holy Place. The reason for this is that what is regarded as the equivalent of the incense altar is not found in the Holy Place but in the outer court of the temple. There is situated the bronze altar that is in front of the Holy Place. That large altar, on which the sacrifices were offered, is the basis for everything. The outer court itself represents the world, but the world seen in the light of the Holy Place, thus part and parcel of the sacredness of it all. In that world the sacrificial animal dies; there *adam* suffers the death penalty; there the terrifying power of the flaming sword is revealed, the tool of death that once caused Adam to flee from the Tree of Life. That altar in the outer court is the reason the church exists. The church can only be in the world because that altar backs her up and carries her. The church stands in this world with the cross at her back. The cross is her ground of being. Only out of the cross can she radiate light and life, and only then can the result be adoration and worship in everything she thinks and does.

The Holy Place is indeed the church's domain: the church has her place there; she lives out her priestly function there; her light shines there; and she dedicates her life to God there. But the Holy Place could not be there if the altar were not in the outer court of the Temple and if the cross were not planted in the world. Because of that, the church now breathes in the pure atmosphere of the Holy Place. She is no longer in the world, but she is not yet in paradise. She is in between these two, and she longs for the moment when the entire world will be paradise and she may appear before God's face.

CHAPTER 3

The Kingdom

The Kingdom Concept

The concept of the kingdom of God resounds like a majestic chorale through the Bible, from Genesis to Revelation. The Psalms, especially, sometimes tremble with ecstasy when they extol this kingdom:

> A mighty God is the Lord,
> A Great King above all gods.
> In his hands are the depths of the earth;
> The heights of the mountains are his.
> To him belongs the sea, for he made it,
> And the dry land shaped by his hands.
> (Ps. 95:3-5; The Grail Psalms)

The prophets also often have trouble finding enough words to express their true kingdom feelings:

> Do you not know?
> Have you not heard?
> Has it not been told you from the beginning?
> Have you not understood since the earth was founded?
> He sits enthroned above the circle of the earth, and its people
>   are like grasshoppers.
> He stretches out the heavens like a canopy,
>   and spreads them out like a tent to live in. (Isa. 40:21-22)

This kingdom concept can already be found in the very first chapter of the Bible. Genesis 1 uses very plain terms to speak of the majesty of God, who by his word called the heavens and the earth into being. Psalm 33:9 simply says, "He spoke and it came to be, he commanded and it sprang into being."

The concept of the kingdom contains a number of elements that are of the highest significance for our inquiry. In the first place, we must realize that God's kingdom has a cosmic character, which means that it comprises the entire world as we have come to know it. Not only are we humans part of that kingdom, but it also includes the worlds of animals and plants. Even the angels are part of this wider context: they too have a place in the harmonious totality of God's kingdom.

This implies that all parts of the world are attuned to each other. Nowhere is there a false note, a dissonance that disturbs the unity, because everything fits harmoniously into the greater scheme of the totality. This applies to each individual specimen but equally to the various circles or spheres found in creation. The celestial bodies follow their orderly trajectories and do so according to God's royal will, obeying his voice. The stars in their courses sound a melodious note in the great concert in which all creatures participate. The mountains rise up high above the water-saturated earth, their proud summits piercing the clouds; yet even these mountains are nothing but servants of him who has planted and secured them by his power. On every page the Bible makes plain that the meaning of creation resides only in the one overarching motif: God's kingdom. That is why Scripture and creation are never at odds. They always form a unity where the one reinforces the other.

> The heavens proclaim the glory of God, and the firmament
>   shows forth the work of his hands.
> Day unto day takes up the story, and night unto night
>   makes known the message. (Ps. 19:2-3)

> The Lord has set his sway in heaven and his kingdom rules over all.
> Give thanks to the Lord, all his angels, mighty in power,
>   fulfilling his word, heeding the voice of his word.
> Give thanks to the Lord, all his hosts, his servants who do his will.

Give thanks to the Lord, all his works, in every place where he rules. My soul, give thanks to the Lord.

(Ps. 103:19-22)

Nowhere in the Bible do we find the word "harmony," but the idea of synergy, of concordance, is one of the most essential features of the entire doctrine of creation found in the Bible. And that synergy can only be so totally harmonious because every part in that great edifice of creation is, in its deepest sense, focused on the one common goal: devout obedience to the will of the Almighty, in which men and women, angels and animals, plants and stars, sun and moon are united. The world in which we live is a well-ordered world. We read in Scripture that God was very pleased when he saw what he had made: "And behold, it was very good" (Gen. 1:31).

The nature of the kingdom of God was not intended to be static but dynamic. It was not destined to continue forever in the same shape and form. On the contrary, from its very inception the kingdom contained an incentive to develop, perfect, and unfold all of its potential and the powers contained in it. This means that from its very beginning the concept of history was entailed in the idea of the kingdom. When we say "kingdom," we say history. The total reality of the kingdom could only become manifest in history. From the very first day of creation, the kingdom had the full range of powerful options. It contained possibilities that would require a slow process to come to full fruition. The entire process, however, was subject to God's will.

All of this also implies that whoever mentions history, mentions humanity. We, the human race, are predestined to fulfill a distinctive calling in that history; as humanity, we are assigned an exceptional place in the greater context of the kingdom from the very first. We are simultaneously *subjects* and to some extent *co-rulers*, viceroys over certain regions. Not everything is subjected to us: we are not given authority over the course of the stars and the planets or the tides of the never-resting seas. But the earth and its plants and animals have been assigned to us, given for us to rule over and to use for God's service, to fathom and understand creation's hidden powers, and so to bring to full development the innate possibilities of creation. That is the meaning of the cultural calling allotted to us immediately after creation (Gen. 1:28-29). Imagine those two humans, feeble man and woman, creatures among creatures, two tiny bits of the universe endowed with self-knowledge, two tiny bits of a world that had become self-conscious. There they were, not even in control of their own heartbeat. There they stood, fragile and weak members of that overwhelming massive context of the kingdom. But also, there they stood as rulers, as princes and princesses among all creatures:

> When I see the heavens, the work of your hands,
> The moon and the stars which you arranged,
> What is man that you should keep him in mind,
> Mortal man that you care for him?
> Yet you have made him little less than a god;
> With glory and honor you crowned him,
> Gave him power over the works of your hand,
> Put all things under his feet. (Ps. 8:4-7)

The Sin against the Kingdom

Our sin has several aspects. There is a priestly moment in sin: we have made ourselves God's equals; we have proclaimed ourselves gods and by that act have abandoned our fellowship with him; we have withdrawn from his influence and have turned our backs on God. That is why we were banished from paradise, because where God dwells there is no place for a second god, nor is there room for those who regard themselves as gods.

However, sin has yet another facet, directly related to the kingdom. To sin is to trespass against God's law, to renounce obedience to God, and to abandon his all-encompassing rule. Sin is actually rebellion, the revolt of the co-rulers against the Supreme King, something the Bible treats with special emphasis. We have crowned ourselves kings. We have taken charge of our lives and have refused to take God's law to heart. By rebutting the will of God, we have caused the entire world order to plunge into chaos. The prophets at times spoke with deep sadness about this revolt, about how the human race had broken away from the harmonious unity of the universe and chosen to go its own way. "Even the stork in the sky knows her appointed seasons, and the dove, the swift and the thrush observe the time of their migration. But my people do not know the requirements of the Lord" (Jer. 8:7). We have ruptured the kingdom and have brought dissonance into the world order. At one time, everything in heaven and on earth was united in one overarching purpose, in devout submission to God, who created it all. We now have excluded ourselves from this goal. The heavens declare God's glory, and the expanse tells us the work of his hands; but we, the human race — we alone have refused to be included in that act of worship. We have torn ourselves away from this all-embracing body and have declared ourselves to be sovereign. We have become a law to ourselves and by that act have clothed ourselves with the mantle of loneliness, no longer able to hear and understand the song of creation; sadly, we are no longer, in turn, seen by creation as part and parcel of it.

We can well imagine that this sundering of creational harmony and rupturing of the kingdom has automatically entailed a host of disastrous consequences. "Cursed is the ground because of you," God says to Adam and Eve (Gen. 3:17). The apostle Paul elaborated on this when he wrote, "For the creation was subject to frustration, not by its own choice, but by the will of the one who subjected it" (Rom. 8:20). Indeed, a curse came over the world when creation was subjected to damnation. Once sin affected just one portion of that beautifully holistic order, it infected its totality, ruining the entire realm. Now its harmonious consonance is no longer a living reality. God himself surrendered his world to the powers of vanity and allowed it to be subject to destruction. God himself took this fateful step because we, humans, wanted to be kings, because we refused to live in a world — even in God's marvelous kingdom — that wants to be subject to him alone.

We are now faced with a development in creation that we cannot understand and control, but of which we daily experience the terrifying consequences. We now see God's work of art embroiled in the power of demons. Satanic forces have thrown themselves onto nature, onto us humans, onto the entire radiant creation. Nowhere does the Bible elaborate on these matters, but once in a while it allows us a peek into the abyss of sorrow and hardship now evident everywhere. This is especially evident in the Gospels. When Peter's mother-in-law suffered from a fever, Jesus "rebuked" the illness and "it left her" (Luke 4:39). When Jesus and his disciples were at sea and a severe storm endangered the ship, Jesus "rebuked" the wind and said to the sea, "Be still!" (Mark 4:39). The forces behind that storm and that fever were satanic; the world of hideous demons played a blasphemous role in those phenomena. Jesus shows us here a scenario regarding life in general (awesome storms) and what will affect us in particular (mysterious diseases), both with ominous consequences. No longer is our universe one of only beauty and harmony; especially in our day, it is one of unpredictable powers that threaten us with annihilation from all directions. The world in which we live is dominated by demons, and we experience the terrible influence of this satanic situation every hour.

It is impossible to visualize the immense difference between the majestic, harmonious unity of creation as it emerged from God's hand and the frantic, demon-dominated planet in which we, cursed humanity, dwell after the Fall into sin. That the kingdom is shattered is the profound tragedy confronting the life of the world. This goes far beyond the fact that we have torn up its cohesion. It actually means that God has surrendered his own creation to Satan and his followers, whose only purpose is to abuse it and destroy it. The kingdom, after all, is made up of all plants, all animals, all people, all angels — all things. The kingdom includes the sea and the land, the mountains and the valleys, all that was and is and is to come — all of it incorporated into a great and mighty whole. The kingdom is the place where all things are in their rightful place and where everything can fulfill its function and work toward its potential in complete harmony with all that surrounds it. The kingdom is synonymous with light, peace, joy, service to God — all in harmonious veneration. Where the kingdom is being destroyed, where this structure comes apart at the seams, there is decomposition, brokenness, fragmentation, enmity, contradiction, meaninglessness, darkness, death. The kingdom is the smile of God's good pleasure: "See, it was very good." With the breaking of the kingdom, God hides his face. Psalm 104:29 says: "When you hide your face, they are terrified." The glow fades away, and something akin to the pall of death covers the world.

It is in this rudderless world that we must carry out our mandate: "Fill the earth and subdue it. Rule over the fish of the sea and the birds of the air and over every living creature that moves on the ground" (Gen. 1:28). A hopeless business! No longer is it service to God, but it has become dire necessity. No longer is the task "by the sweat of your brow you will serve your God"; rather, it is now "by the sweat of your brow you will eat your food" (Gen. 3:19). It has become slavery. We, the human race, have no choice but to develop the world, lest we perish in this world. We think and toil and delve and do, and in all this we are in chains. Job 7:1 knows this: "Does not man have hard service on earth, and are his days not like those of a hired man?" Sometimes we look up, suddenly frightened in the midst of our sorrowful labor, and we wonder what is the sense of everything we do. The entire book of Ecclesiastes is one heart-rending cry about the futility of life seen in the perspective of the brokenness of the kingdom. Everything that once was beautiful is now to be pitied and without hope.

Yes, we can do mighty things, and we can penetrate the secrets of creation; but it really no longer makes sense because we can no longer build a harmonious world. We can never restore its disorder. War after war is destroying its existence. The richest cultural treasures, constructed with great effort and care, are reduced to rubble under the weight of the curse that threatens all human life. There is no escaping it. Whatever we do is no longer ennobled by the wonderful perspective that someday in the future a perfect and harmonious world will be born. Our life has turned into a flight to the bomb shelters. We have retreated into the caves of our knowing and thinking with no other purpose than to safeguard ourselves from the calamities that threaten us from all sides. Through all this we increasingly try to maintain our own self-importance, and, in a strong desire to make up for what we have lost, we put on a brave front, and we try, almost desperately, to fend off disappointment and discouragement.

God's Great Plan

Nevertheless, God did not abandon his kingdom concept. On the contrary, he opted for an even greater and more conspicuous version. The kingdom concept has become the most pronounced motif of the history of the world, which from now on is all about the emergence, the new birth, of the kingdom.

This kingdom that God is busy realizing has a very particular character. If we wish to fathom its superb beauty to some degree, we must point out some of its features. In the first place, the kingdom of God is depicted in the Bible as a reality of the end-time. Of course, in the dispensation of the present world, the kingdom is always *in statu nascendi* (always being born); it is always "near," but in reality it will only be there when all the strands of world history come together again at the end-time. That kingdom was there already in the *Urzeit*, and straight through the rubble and ruins of history it will again be manifested before our very eyes as an overwhelmingly magnificent reality. The eschatological nature of the kingdom is one of the first characteristics that is striking us.

This eschatological feature is expressed in the Old Testament in all kinds of ways. Especially in the second part of the prophecy of Isaiah, the glorious future of the kingdom forms the central theme that dominates all other aspects. Its main premise is that on the great day of the Lord, in the end-time, the Lord God will reveal his kingly power: on that day he will permanently expel all decaying and destructive forces that have penetrated his creation. On that day the indescribable glory of the new reality of the eternal kingdom will appear in living color, a reality in which all things will again have their rightful place. Nowhere is this future better outlined than in Paul's profound description in Ephesians 1:9-10, where he speaks of "the mystery of his will," which is to be "put into effect when the times will have reached their fulfillment — to bring all things in heaven and on earth together under one head, even Christ." There we find the Old Testament prophecy shorn of all poetic embellishment as a simple description of what God intends to realize for this broken world. It fits in perfectly with the eschatological perspective of the kingdom that it takes priority over all other matters in the Bible. The covenant of grace, for instance, finds its deepest meaning in the coming kingdom. So does the coming of Jesus Christ into the world, which, when seen in the light of Scripture, has as its sole intention the restoration of the kingdom. Christ's suffering and death — indeed, the entire order of redemption — has no other purpose than the realization of the kingdom. Grace itself is not there for its own sake. The central point of the gospel is not us poor humans and our pain and suffering; rather, its entire focus is aimed at the unique and powerful reality that God wants to reinstate his kingdom.

It is God's intention to unite all fractured parts of his creation into one overarching harmony. There is no such thing as individual salvation. All salvation is of necessity universal. The goal of our life can never be that we personally may enjoy God and be saved in him. The goal of our life can only be that we again become part of the wider context of the kingdom of God, where all things are again unified under the one and only all-wise will of him who lives and rules for ever.

In the third place, our attention should be focused on Jesus Christ, in whom the kingdom is realized. All the strands of history converge in him. Just as Adam's sin shattered the world, so it will again become an organic unity in Christ. Christ is not only the priest who has restored for us the way back to communion with God, but he is also the king who establishes his saving rule over this fallen world. When he appears, says John the Baptizer, "the kingdom of heaven is near" (Matt. 3:2), and when Jesus himself starts to preach the gospel in Judea and Galilee, his initial message is none other than the single proclamation that "the kingdom of heaven is near" (Matt. 4:17). Through his suffering and death, Christ reinstated the kingdom and united in himself all things under God's rule, including Jesus' miracles. When he healed the sick, raised the dead, and rebuked the demons, he demonstrated that all the strands of world history converge in him. It has never been the burden of Scripture that the kingdom would be confined to the human race. No, the kingdom is always universal and cosmic in scope, benefiting the entire creation. In fact, Christ, in his authority over storm and sea, demonstrates that, in him, God's kingship embraces the entire world, which would be meaningless without him. The three great kingdom metaphors in the New Testament — the one related in the synoptic Gospels about the kingdom of heaven, the other in the Gospel of John about the vine and its branches, and the last one in the letters of Paul about the body of Christ and "being in Christ" — all are interpretations of the one truth that in Christ all things are gathered together into one body.

In 1 Corinthians, Paul expresses himself as follows: "Then the end will come, when he hands over the kingdom to God the Father after he has destroyed all dominion, authority and power: for he must reign until he has put all his enemies under his feet. When he has done this, then the Son himself will be made subject to him who put everything under him, so that God may be all in all" (1 Cor. 15:24-28).

It is at this point that the kingdom of God enters the medium of history. It does not suddenly, as if by magic, spring up out of the ground, but it arises and develops gradually. That is the reason why such a large part of the Bible consists of historical books. Other religions have not, as a rule, paid attention to history and its problems because they have not detected the line of history. The Bible, however, incorporates history in God's dealings with the world and shows us that the meaning of history lies in the concept of the kingdom of God.

The Old Testament emphasizes that the kingdom of Yahweh is prefigured in the nation of Israel, which was both church and nation, uniting in itself the priestly and the kingly office, which is the reason it was called a "priestly kingdom" (Exod. 19:6). On the sacred mountain of Jerusalem the temple sat adjacent to the royal palace, the reason why Mount Zion was the name for both.

The national character of Israel's religion was one of the most enigmatic and painful periods in the life of the church of ancient times. The church, being a nation, had a place amid the other countries and was thus also part of the political developments of the world at that time. She suffered humiliation, was involved in waging war, was attacked by large kingdoms, and was conquered and taken into exile. Thus the church, as nation, had to carry out her dual task in the world of that day. That the church totally coincided with the nation was a strong indication that this dual role pointed to the coming of God's kingdom. God wanted to establish a kingdom in the world and preserve it despite all opposition. This preservation often occurred in miraculous ways when the odds looked impossible. God insisted on this role in Israel's history, which often proved quite burdensome. When, as a nation, Israel left God's ways and assumed the customs of other peoples, God allowed it to go under. And after much suffering and exile, God pulled them up again out of their misery and raised them safely above the tensions and turmoil of the world. Israel's history perfectly portrays the history of the kingdom.

At times Israel itself was fully aware of this. The national dream was that God, in due course, would unite all peoples and nations under his rule. Then, in that hour of redemption that was bound to come, all idol worshipers would cease their opposition to Israel's God and come to worship in Jerusalem. "The Lord will be king over the whole earth. On that day there will be one Lord, and his name the only name" (Zech. 14:9). "Then the survivors from all the nations that have attacked Jerusalem will go up year after year to worship the King, the Lord Almighty, and to celebrate the Feast of Tabernacles" (Zech. 14:16). Isaiah sees the coming glory of the kingdom in the form of a banquet prepared for all nations. It is there, on Mount Zion, that God will destroy "the shroud that enfolds all peoples, the sheet that covers all nations" (Isa. 25:7). Whenever Israel would become quite emotional about that day, the day when the house of David would rule the entire world, this emotion was not a distorted expression of a deep-rooted nationalism, but it stemmed from the profound conviction that only the heavenly kingdom of Yahweh would prevail and that all peoples in the world would at one time be united under that banner.

The basis of Israel's existence was the kingdom concept, a concept that dominates the whole of Scripture from the first page to the last. The ultimate reason for the dramatic tensions and turmoil in the history of the world lies exactly there. Nothing is further from the truth than the idea that God realizes his kingdom along lines of quiet development. The truth is that God's kingdom comes by battling hostile powers from beginning to end. Why? Because throughout history there have always been secular powers that merge to form empires which, upon closer inspection, have no other goal than to establish a human kingdom, a kingdom where deified man celebrates his triumphs. In other words, the kingdom of God has a terrible rival: the empire of humanity.

That empire is the opposite of God's kingdom. It, too, wants unity and order; it, too, wants harmony. However, this harmony is not geared to communal obedience and devout service to God; rather, it aims at collective self-deification, which is the root of sin. The empire of humanity has as its most basic aim the shared desire to construct an orderly world, but a world without God, in total disregard of him. That human empire is an imitation of God's plan: it is an attempt, by hook or by crook, to rob God of his great plan and thus to try to make God's plan come true through human culture.

There are numerous instances in world history of this kind of human kingdom. For a while it was evident in the Babylonian and Persian empires, and later in Greece and Rome. Common to all these is the stubborn delusion that the empire has divine attributes, that the king or emperor possesses divine qualities, and that the people as a whole embody divine powers. That is, the empire is God. In more recent history this same imperial notion was present in all kinds of political and imperial structures and notions. People rely on a Führer, or a divine emperor, as a visible symbol of the invisible unity of the people or the race. People want to see themselves reflected in such a Führer, want to lose themselves in their misplaced ecstasy of faith in their own divine greatness. World history is nothing but the ever-repeated attempt to build empires and the stubborn striving to rediscover humans' lost unity in such an empire.

However, sooner or later all these efforts are doomed to fail. God simply will not allow his plan to be played out by others. The empire tries to combine all powers into one comprehensive whole, but it is unable to reach or even approach that lofty goal. We must not forget that sin always leads to disintegration and fragmentation, which makes it impossible even for an all-out communal effort to succeed. Sin simply means destruction, and, based on this societal tendency to destruction, it is impossible to erect a world empire. The tragedy of world history lies exactly there: the consolidation of mighty imperial powers leads to violent conflicts, terrible wars, chaos, and destruction. Attempts to unify the empire internally into an organic whole bring about persecution and ever-larger concentration camps; they lead to torture and elimination of everything that does not fit into the empire's communal goal, all of which ends up in tyranny and boundless intolerance. Every attempt to bring the human kingdom into being is doomed to futility. The book of Daniel sees this displayed symbolically. In chapter 7, Daniel sees the lives of the nations in the form of misshapen animals rising out of the churning sea, all of them identified with world empires and all perishing because they lack substance.

The human kingdom is a utopia, an idealistic impossibility, something that is and is not, something that arises but can never last. Building the Tower of Babel fails every time it is attempted (Gen. 11). Over against all these kingdoms God makes his own kingdom come. Those human empires resist God's plan with every fiber of their being; they act like demons in their fuming rage against God's intention. "The kings of the earth take their stand and the rulers gather together against the Lord and against his anointed one" (Ps. 2:2). Indeed, these kings were repeatedly destroyed with an iron scepter and beaten into pieces like a potter's vessel. Recent history has again been a most horrendous confirmation of this. The history of God's kingdom is no quiet, placid stream; it is charged with dramatic upheavals. It grinds and grates against the manifestations of human kingdoms, and at every moment it points to the overwhelming end, the finale of world history, the great day of the Lord.

When we observe these two opponents, the palace and the Temple, they speak of two different worlds. Both have a close connection to *Urzeit* and end-time, but they do so in very different ways. The Temple is paradise, a hidden reality in the midst of the world. The Temple is the *Urzeit*, which always remains real, and is at the same time the end-time, pointing to the paradise of God and the streams of living water. The Temple is the meeting place of the beginning and the end, where there are no hours, no days, no years, no decades or centuries. This is the sphere of the eternal, where the clock of time no longer ticks, the humdrum of world history is no longer heard, and we are embraced by what is unchangeable. In the Temple the priest stands beyond history; he is Adam himself, representing the imperishable in us. This is where Adam is, returning as he does to the Tree of Life with head bowed, counting on God's grace in Jesus Christ. Here he stands, age in and age out, defying the storms of world history. In the Temple we hear the explanation of our eternal mystery through the tender symbolism of God's revelation.

The king, too, stands between *Urzeit* and end-time, but he is on another plane. He stands amidst the turbulent events of history, right in the middle of the dramatic tensions of our time. The king has gone beyond the kingdom of the *Urzeit*, and before him lies the kingdom of the end, far beyond the horizon. He stands in between the beginning and the end, in the center of the awesome struggle God's kingdom is waging in the world. He stands in the history that is the meaning of his life. History ceases in the Temple. This is where eternity whispers, while in the palace the roar of history rumbles on from year to year.

King and priest operate on different planes; they cannot be compared. Adam dwells on both, and on both we hear the gentle song of the beginning of all things. The first murmur of the new day is also present on both planes, the great day of Yahweh, when he will be all and in all.

CHAPTER 4

Christ, the Central Focus of Scripture

The Bible Proclaims Christ

The Bible is not a collection of individual books but comes to us as a single entity, the book of God's revelation, of which Christ is the central focus. That is why we can say that the entire Bible, both the Old and the New Testaments, proclaims Christ. That does not mean, of course, that the Old Testament believers were always fully aware of this and thus looked forward to Christ's coming. It is even very much a question of whether the Old Testament saints really grasped that the entire Temple worship was focused on the Messiah, who would come at a future date. At any rate, the question whether they anticipated Christ is a matter that we will investigate later. What really matters for us is that *God's* focus in the Old Testament is Christ. Both in the temple ceremonies and the prophecies, the Messiah figure emerges more clearly and sharply all the time, showing that God was slowly and carefully preparing his people for the coming of the Redeemer.

It is completely in line with the history of divine revelation that in the old dispensation the coming Messiah is pictured especially as priest and king. Israel existed in a dual capacity, being both church and nation. It was a church operating as a nation and, as such, had two centers: the Temple and the city of Jerusalem. Both were located on Mount Zion, around which the nation of Israel was situated in its dual capacity. Two key figures ruled over Israel, the high priest and the king; together, they dominated the national scene. Therefore, it is not surprising that the anticipated Messiah is pictured as both, since he is simultaneously both priest and king. The coming "branch" will be "clothed with majesty and will sit and rule on his throne [indicating his kingship]: thus the throne will be occupied by a priest. And there will be harmony between the two [between his royal and his priestly office]" (Zech. 6:13). Thus will both focal points of Israel's being as a nation be present in one person: Christ will unite Temple and palace.

We might wonder whether the Old Testament also celebrates the Messiah as prophet. It is undoubtedly true that the office of prophet of the coming Christ receives some attention, but the prophetic office is not emphasized nearly as much as are those of king and priest. That's because prophets were figures of much less importance in Israel's existence; in reality, they were not much in the picture of the life of the old church. As we have seen before, religious instruction was the task of the priests, so under normal circumstances there was no need for a prophet; hence he normally appears only when something abnormal happens. This would be the case when the priests fail to instruct the people or the king leads the nation astray. It is then that the prophet emerges from his hiding place. It is then that his powerful preaching calls the apostate king to order and threatens the nation with destruction unless the people repent. The prophet appears on the scene only when the situation for Israel as both nation and church has become dire. The prophet is thus an extraordinary figure in Israel's history. In the course of its existence, Israel does not have a third central focus in addition to palace and temple — that of the prophetic office — because this function is a divine corrective for the first two: it sits in judgment on both king and priest. That explains the place of the prophet in Israel's life as a nation, and it explains why the Messiah's prophetic office receives less attention than do the other two, which belonged to the usual life of the church.

When we start to visualize these two offices (which the prophets attributed to Christ) for a moment, a new world opens up for us. The Messiah is priest, that is, "Son of man," humanity personified, *adam* (Dan. 7:13). He dwells in the realm of the eternal, of that which never changes. He stands where *Urzeit* and end-time approach each other, outside the boundaries of history. He represents the eternal humanness: as such, he enters paradise, goes into the Temple, and draws near to God's throne. Yet his being a king means that he resides in the center of history, where God's plan for the world unfolds. He stands in the place between the breakup of the kingdom through sin and the healing of the kingdom at the end of time. There he stands, dead center, at the very place where God restores the kingdom through him and in him. There he gathers all the world's nations under his authority; there he makes the entire cosmos in all her strata subject to him, and, once he has accomplished this — when the world is once again in total harmony — he will place it at the feet of God the Father.

The Messiah is the priest forever, but in the manner of Melchizedek, the man without father and mother and without genealogy, who is at the same time king of Salem. He intervenes forcefully in the world's events and guides them to the destination appointed by God. That is the wondrous greatness of the Messiah anticipated in the Old Testament.

We can readily assume that both these characteristics of the Messiah were not always obvious. Already in the early days of salvation history, the emphasis was almost exclusively on the royal calling the Messiah would assume at some time. The dying Jacob already prophesies: "The scepter will not depart from Judah, nor the ruler's staff from between his feet, until he to whom it belongs comes, and the obedience of the nations is his" (Gen. 49:10). It is clear from this that the Messiah will be king. All nations will be subject to him as he makes this broken world into a unified whole, in devout obedience to the Lord God. In fact, this entire concept is already evident in God's promise in Genesis 3:15: "And I will put enmity between you and the woman, and between your offspring and hers; he will crush your head, and you will strike his heel." There, too, the coming Messiah is painted as the great victor, the one who will heal the schism, undo the curse that afflicts the world because of sin, and thus free the world from the overpowering demonic forces.

It is impractical to cite the numerous Old Testament texts in which the coming Messiah is sketched in his royal status. Suffice it to say that these king prophecies always have an eschatological character: they always refer to the end-time, the great day that will come when God restores the order of this world. The Messiah-King is none other than the messenger of the Lord God, the one who represents him in this world and makes it subject to his authority.

Let me add at once that these "king prophecies" are always universal in scope. They never refer to the restoration of Israel alone, nor do they concern the destruction of the pagan powers as such; but they are always aimed at salvation for the world, the salvation that will be its portion when the entire world, in an intimate embrace of God's chosen people, will bow down before the God of Israel and recognize him as the God of the whole earth. That means that God has rich promises in store even for those pagan nations. However, the pagan principle, centered as it is on the notion of self-deification, will have to be totally eradicated, for idolatry cannot exist on God's holy mountain.

It is clear that the Messiah-King has the authority to judge. He is not only a king, but above all a judge. He will subdue all ungodly, diabolical powers and will establish God's authority over this world. The day of his coming will be a terrible day. "But who can endure the day of his coming? Who can stand when he appears? For he will be like a refiner's fire or a launderer's soap.... Surely the day is coming; it will burn like a furnace.... See, I will send you the prophet Elijah before that great and dreadful day of the Lord comes" (Mal. 3:2; 4:1, 5). In the nature of the case, that judgment will in the first place affect the nations: "He will judge between the nations and will settle disputes for many peoples" (Isa. 2:4). But Israel will not escape that judgment either, and there, too, the Messiah will exercise his office as judge.

And the outcome will be a new world in which the order of nature will be altered. Then the breach now evident in all strata of creation will have been bridged. "In that day I will make a covenant for them with the beasts of the field and the birds of the air and the creatures that move along the ground. Bow and sword and battle I will abolish from the land, so that all may lie down in safety" (Hosea 2:18). Then the nations "will beat their swords into plowshares and their spears into pruning hooks. Nation will not take up sword against nation, nor will they train for war anymore. Every man will sit under his own vine and under his own fig tree" (Mic. 4:3-4).

The prophecy of Isaiah especially outlines, in no uncertain terms, this entirely new and marvelous character of the kingdom of the Messiah: "Then the Lord will create over all of Mount Zion and over those who assemble there a cloud of smoke by day and a glow of flaming fire by night; over all the glory will be a canopy" (Isa. 4:5-6). Therefore, the kingdom that is to come is cosmic in scope: it concerns not only us humans but draws the whole creation within its jurisdiction. Thus it is no surprise that the prophet can hardly find words enough to express how he pictures the Messiah and his glory. Take Isaiah 9:5: "And he will be called Wonderful Counselor, Mighty God, Everlasting Father, Prince of Peace." Those words portray the coming Messiah-King in all his glory, the one who will restore this world — so confused, so ripped apart, so possessed by demons — and will unify it. He will transform it into God's kingdom.

At the same time we repeatedly encounter biblical texts that point to the Messiah as *priest*. Besides the aforementioned Psalm 110, the songs of the Servant of the Lord especially come to mind; they are found in the second part of the prophecy of Isaiah, particularly chapter 53: "But he was pierced for our transgressions, he was crushed for our iniquities; the punishment that brought us peace was upon him, and by his wounds we are healed.... He was oppressed and afflicted, yet he did not open his mouth.... Yet it was the Lord's will to crush him and cause him to suffer, and though the Lord makes his life a guilt offering, he will see his offspring and prolong his days, and the will of the Lord will prosper in his hand" (Isa. 53:5, 7, 10).

When we read these words, we cannot help but be reminded of the priest who enters the Holy of Holies carrying blood, a sign that he has gone through death. The Messiah is Adam, who, having died, returns to paradise. We find similar "priestly" passages particularly in the prophecies of Haggai and Zechariah, spoken when the new Temple was being built. The Messiah will restore the Temple; in him God will again live in the midst of his people. He is the great high priest Joshua, who embodies God's presence among the people.

Our conclusion must be that, even though the royal aspect usually predominates in the Old Testament prophecies, we can also notice the priestly features of the coming Messiah. He will take his place in history, while at the same time rising above history, where we find treasures that will never perish.

The Life of Jesus

All these Old Testament perceptions also resonate in the New Testament, where the Messiah is depicted in the greatness of his actions. It stands to reason that, as a rule, the expectations with which believers in Jesus' day approached him lay in the sphere of history. John the Baptizer had already announced the Messiah as the great judge-king: "His winnowing fork is in his hand, and he will clear his threshing floor, gathering his wheat into the barn and burning up the chaff with unquenchable fire" (Matt. 3:12). The Messiah occupies a distinct place in history: as the end-time dawns, when the world has become totally chaotic and after terrible judgments, he will restore God's kingdom.

In Jesus' life itself, the unfolding of his royal stature takes place in gradual and wonderful ways. It is impossible to cite every detail, so I will limit myself to a few momentous occasions. We should note first of all that the main content of Jesus' proclamation, especially in the beginning, is concerned with the kingdom of heaven. It is extremely unfortunate that the concept of the kingdom of heaven or the kingdom of God has escaped our dogmatic reflection and is paid scant attention in our Christian life. That is why we find it very difficult to read the Good News with that wonderful suspense that comes from seeing it against the backdrop of the overwhelming reality of the kingdom of God. The kingdom of God has come "near" in Christ: the great day of the Lord is about to come. The kingdom claims the entire cosmos in all its manifestations. Wherever Jesus comes, the demons flee, the fever subsides, the sea becomes calm, and the storm obeys. The kingdom of God has come near, and leprosy retreats, the blind open their eyes in utter amazement, the lame start to leap in spontaneous enthusiasm, and the dead rise from their graves. Indeed, the kingdom of God is near. All those shattering, destructive, depressing, and disruptive forces now dominating the universe fly away in despair and anguish as soon as the king appears. All those miracle stories recorded in the Gospels, which we in our thoughts and our daily lives find difficult to explain and which we can only deal with if we somehow spiritualize them, are clearly meant to manifest the awesome powers of the Messiah in his kingdom. As such, they serve as proof that God will not surrender this terrible world to the powers of decay at work in it, but that the great day in which he himself will gather up his world into a harmonious symphony of adoration has begun. Christ's miracles gather the kingdom under a cosmic umbrella. The kingdom is the restoration of the *Urzeit*; it is the introduction of the eventual "renewal" (Matt. 19:28).

In Jesus' verbal teaching he approaches the kingdom from a completely different angle. His foremost emphasis is on the strict adherence that the kingdom requires of all who want to participate in it. The kingdom is completely different from participating in an earthly empire, different even from the theocratic rules of David and Solomon, which could only be faint reflections of the messianic kingdom. God's kingdom requires total commitment, the totality of our thoughts and lives; it leaves no room for even one sinful notion or inclination. If we want to be part of the harmonious community of God's kingdom, then we may not harbor secret thoughts of hatred or jealousy toward our neighbor, nor may we in the recesses of our mind commit adultery. Rather, with everything that is ours, with heart and soul, we are to surrender to the majesty of the kingdom. In that kingdom there is only room for absolute norms; we can enter there only with head bowed, poor in spirit, without a trace of hubris or self-will. That kingdom is visible when the requirement is the radical practice of moral relationships; it calls for such a high level of perfection that we tremble before the impossible holiness of such a standard. Imagine this: we have to be perfect — that is, of a piece, whole, without an iota of dualism or brokenness, radical and absolute — "as our Father in heaven is perfect" (Matt. 5:48). In the realm of secular relationships, where everything is based on relative virtues, the kingdom represents an unworldly abnormality, sheer foolishness, something that cannot be. And that's true. We have to pluck out the eye that wants to seduce us to sin; we must be willing to cut off our hand, give up all we hold dear, surrender well-being and life itself, if we desire to glimpse something of the kingdom. But once we have seen it, our heart trembles with infinite joy over the glorious future that God has reserved for us and the world. We can enjoy this future only by undergoing a "rebirth," because only through "a personal experience of being born again" are we able to witness the great "rebirth" of all that is and moves and has its being. Once we have gained that insight, it is not difficult to surrender without any reservations. "This is worth more to me than anything else," we will say.

It is not surprising that the kingdom that Jesus proclaims, sometimes in the most hard-hitting terms, assails every ounce of hubris and selfishness so common in all of us. The conversations Jesus had with the scribes and Pharisees prove this beyond a shadow of a doubt. Matthew 23 in particular, where Jesus repeatedly says to them, "Woe to you," shows unsparingly that those of us who want to preserve even a small part of our sinful self, who stubbornly cling to the idea of self-redemption, do not have a ghost of a chance of entering the kingdom. In the future world order that is to be established by Jesus, their only escape will be to slink away and hide themselves in "outer darkness." These terrible words, which appear in the Gospels on several occasions, are so loaded with fear and trembling that we shudder when we think about them deeply at all. Outside the "kingdom" is not a vacuum of nothingness, but the thoroughly fearsome area of "outer darkness."

Thus, throughout the entire period of Jesus' wanderings on earth, we repeatedly encounter the concept of the kingdom and the royal status of the Messiah. There are a few instances where this emerges quite distinctly and where it dominates the entire event, for example, the devil's temptation of Jesus in the desert, particularly in what Matthew calls the third temptation (Matt. 4:8): "Again the devil took him to a very high mountain and showed him all the kingdoms of the world and their splendor. All this I will give you if you bow down and worship me." At stake here is the preeminent question of whether it is possible for us to realize the kingdom in this world without God. Might it be possible to fasten this ripped-apart world together, to unite this torn world into a harmonious whole through human effort alone, and thus to construct a kingdom made by us? We might call this notion of the devil the führer idea. Paying attention to the authority Jesus has, we could say that, if there were one führer in world history capable of founding such a "Reich," then it would have to be Jesus. In such an empire all powers would be mobilized and everything would be "coordinated." There would be only one worldview, one socioeconomic system, one educational philosophy, one religion, namely, the religion of humanity. That is what the two-dimensional empire would look like, the horizontal empire of this world, without a vertical aspect, without any relationship with God. That is the temptation facing Jesus.

Legend has it that when Gautama the Buddha was born, it was predicted that he was destined to become a *chakravartin*, a world ruler, unless he voluntarily gave up this ideal and desired to become a world teacher. As the story goes, Buddha resisted the temptation to become a *chakravartin* in order to acquaint the world with the true teaching. According to Hastings' *Dictionary of the Bible*, Islam "represents the theocratic idea in a radically secular form": Islam wants to build an empire, but does so by means of a worldly structure. In God's plan, Jesus Christ also had the *chakravartin* temptation placed before him. He was offered a world empire, an empire of majestic scope and massive substance. The offer came to him while he was on a "very high mountain," the ancient world mountain dating back to the *Urzeit*, the core of the world from which all the kingdoms of the world can be seen in one glance. Jesus declined this temptation with vehemence, not because he wanted to be something other than a world ruler, but because he was aware that a world empire, the great kingdom, can only be based on worshiping the true God: "Worship the Lord your God and serve him only." The kingdom cannot be realized in the two-dimensional plane of this world; every attempt to do so would fail miserably. The eternal and imperishable kingdom of God rests only on the unshakable pillar of adoration: "Serve him only." The kingdom can only come in devout obedience to God. (There are still other moments in the Savior's life that clearly portray the kingdom concept, but since these generally take place during the time of his great suffering, it would be better to deal with them later.)

The priestly function of the Messiah does not play as prominent a role in the Gospels as one would expect. In that regard the Gospels follow the lead of the old prophecies. Still, there are numerous places where Christ's priestly dignity is made evident to us. Already in his teenage years, the Savior felt a deep attraction to the Temple service, something we can only gather from the fact that he recognized himself in the Temple. In a few well-chosen words, Luke describes for us how the twelve-year-old Jesus stayed behind in the Temple building after his parents had already departed for home. He then reports that Jesus, when questioned why he had done this, gave the remarkable answer: "Didn't you know I had to be in my Father's house?" (Luke 2:49). In Jesus' affinity with the Temple, we already find the first indication that it was, for him, much more than a simple building where God was honored. The Temple was Jesus himself — that is, his entire existence was embodied in the Temple.

Christ, the Central Focus of Scripture

Later, other matters also became significant. When baptized by John the Baptizer, the Savior said, "It is proper for us to do this to fulfill all righteousness" (Matt. 3:15). The baptism itself meant a total identification of Christ with sinful humanity and the world. He put himself in our place without any hesitation, and he underwent baptism, which unmistakably signified that he submitted to death, because he knew that he was to be totally one with the human race. He was *adam:* humanity in its curse and humiliation, humanity expelled from paradise, the person who, only by undergoing death and going past the flaming sword, could come to the Tree of Life. In his identification with us humans, Jesus would leave no stone unturned. To be one with us, he would fulfill every righteous act, every obligation imposed by God.

His office as priest was shown most dramatically in the episode of the transfiguration on the mountain. That is where time stopped. He was, then and there, elevated above the turmoil of history. On the Mount of Transfiguration we can taste the pure atmosphere of paradise and uninterrupted communion with God. Both Moses and Elijah were there consulting with Jesus, demonstrating that we find ourselves in a milieu where time stands still, where only the eternal values that shape human history count. God himself is there, and so is Adam, who appears before God in the splendor of paradise, in the innermost part of the Temple. On the Mount of Transfiguration the office of priest is displayed to the fullest, in the boundless beauty of communion with God. Only the topic of discussion among Moses, Elijah, and Christ, namely, the "departure which he was about to bring to fulfillment in Jerusalem" (Luke 9:31), was a reminder of the outer temple court, where the sacrifice had yet to be offered.

There were other instances in which the disciples observed some of the glory of the perfect priesthood. Matthew tells us that the disciples, when seeing Jesus' miracles, were reminded of the word of Isaiah: "He took up our infirmities and carried our diseases" (Matt. 8:17). Behind Jesus' royal power, from which the demons flee, the disciples sensed something of his immense suffering: Jesus can only take away diseases because he himself assumes their pain. Nothing in the world disappears just by itself; only through transfer, when Jesus takes upon himself the burden of the world, can we be saved. That is exactly what John the Baptizer expressed in his mysterious words: "Look, the lamb of God who takes away the sin of the world" (John 1:29).

If we wonder in what details the priestly office reveals itself, then we have to limit ourselves to a few telling features. Jesus Christ is Adam. He completely identifies himself with us curse-ridden and doom-burdened humans and takes upon himself humanity's misery. In his weakness and pain, in his fatigue and disappointment, he is Adam — humanity personified. Soon he will be crowned with the thorns, which the Father God has foreshadowed in Genesis 3:18: "The earth will produce thorns and thistles for you," as a token of humanity's curse. Jesus is Adam: *Ecce homo* ("here is the man" [John 19:5]). One of the names Jesus used most often to refer to himself is "Son of man": "The Son of man has no place to lay his head" (Matt. 8:20). His dwelling place is at the edge of paradise, before the gate with the flaming sword. He stands in the *Urzeit*, which has put its stamp on the entire course of history. His year of origin is the *Urzeit*, the beginning, when human life was decided for all ages. We find Jesus in the place to which Adam escaped, clothed in crude animal pelts, on the fringes of God's paradise. There he stands, at the edge of the Temple, at the entrance to the Holy of Holies, where the golden glow of eternity dazzles, and where cherubim decline their heads in never-ending amazement over the cover of the ark of atonement. In that environment Jesus finds his life and his suffering. In that setting we can be found, far outside the drumbeat of world history; there is only the eternal human, only that which endures forever. Jesus Christ is the perfect high priest. Expressed in the language of the covenant, we may all say: "He is you and me; we are included in him; he took your place and mine." (At this juncture I will not go on any further about the priestly office of Christ. Later, when I elaborate in greater specificity on Jesus' suffering, we will repeatedly encounter these different features and will deal with them then.)

The Priest-King Office in the Epistles and in the Revelation of John

We will now take a brief journey through the books of the New Testament to see what they show us about the work of Christ. It is at once clear that

Christ, the Central Focus of Scripture

Paul describes in great detail both the priestly and the kingly character of Christ's work. This is most evident in the beautiful expression "in Christ," which appears frequently in the Pauline Epistles, especially those to the Ephesians and Colossians.

The words "in Christ" are unmistakably of priestly content: "In him we have redemption through his blood" (Eph. 1:7). We are included in Adam, who stands in our place and who is us. But these same words also have a strong royal emphasis. It pleased God, "when the times will have reached their fulfillment, to bring all things in heaven and on earth together under one head, even Christ; in him we were also chosen" (Eph. 1:10-11). The words "in him" point to the end-time, when all strands of world history will be gathered in the hands of Christ, and when the kingdom will be handed over to God the Father. In other words, Paul's typical use of the expression "in him" has a priestly background and is kingly in intent. Paul is also the one who calls Christ *adam*, the "second Adam" (1 Cor. 15:45-47). Christ moves in the plane that rises above history, where the centuries are of no consequence, where the paradise trees flourish and the cherubim threaten. His life does not bear a date; he belongs to another stratum. In him, Adam enters paradise via death and approaches the Tree of Life.

In his Epistle to the Romans, Paul draws a close parallel between Adam and Christ and shows how, in Christ, the strand, broken by Adam, is repaired (Rom. 5:12-21). And now, in that same Adam, we all have reentered paradise. The paradise that in the *Urzeit* was the place where we lived with God — the paradise that has never totally disappeared but has, in the Holy of Holies, always remained with us, even though it was closed to us by heavy curtains — is the paradise where Christ has gone via death. It is now for us, "in him," the place where our real dwelling lies. In Christ, God has given us "a place in the heavenly realms" (Eph. 2:6), and has blessed us "in the heavenly realms with every spiritual blessing in Christ" (Eph. 1:3). We have been lifted out of the world, with its history of totally futile attempts to establish a human kingdom, and we have been transferred to the "kingdom of the Son he loves" (Col. 1:13). We now are firmly rooted in a different situation, far above history, where the paradise river flows and where God himself dwells among us. There we stand, not as solitary figures but intimately connected with each other and also in loving communion with the entire creation, which is now still "groaning as in the pain of childbirth" and longs for the moment when "it will be liberated from its bondage to decay and brought into the glorious freedom of the children of God" (Rom. 8:21-22). In this powerful communion we stand in Christ Jesus as in an indescribably great and magnificent temple in which each person is no more than a building block, a member of a community of people who through the ages "are being built together to become a dwelling in which God lives by his Spirit" (Eph. 2:21-22).

In his Epistles to the Thessalonians, Paul elaborates somewhat more on this struggle, which the kingdom of Christ in our dispensation wages against all demonic and anti-Christian forces, until the kingdom will celebrate total victory in the end. The Epistle to the Hebrews assumes the kingship of Christ, but the remainder of the letter explains in great detail Christ's priestly work after the ordering of Melchizedek: "But when the priest had offered for all time one sacrifice for sins, he sat down at the right hand of God" (Heb. 10:12).

Finally, the Revelation of John takes us to the time of the return of the *Urzeit*, but now in an even more perfect beauty — in Christ Jesus. With breathtaking suspense John pictures the gigantic struggle that the kingdom of Christ has to wage against the powers of the beast and against the false prophet. In frightening scenes he brings to life the different stations of this final struggle, the grand finale of world history. The human empire arises there in hitherto unknown greatness and power, and for a while it seems about to embrace the entire world. Then, however, it bursts like a soap bubble. Proud Babylon collapses; the end of its days has come. Then world history ends in paradise. Again we hear the murmur of the river of living waters; again we stand on a very high mountain, the paradise mount; again we read of the Tree of Life. World history comes full circle. The paradise that was always there, that was actually never totally gone, is back in incomparable beauty. And "the glory of God gives it [the New Jerusalem] light, and the Lamb is its light" (Rev. 21:23). The priestly and kingly offices meet in the end-time, when the terrifying drama ends. Eternity swallows up time and hides it within itself as a secret. The Lamb that was slain, the second Adam — who passed through death into paradise — is able to open up the seven seals, to guide the history of the world to its purpose and destination, its entrance into the eternal and wonderful kingdom of God.

CHAPTER 5

Christ's Arrest

Gethsemane and Eden

The suffering of our Lord Jesus Christ has been described in all four Gospels in great detail. All four authors sensed that they were dealing here with the essence of the work of redemption that was brought about by Christ in this world. That's why all particulars in this matter were judged to be of the greatest importance. That's also why the Gospel writers informed us of even the smallest details of his last days on the *via dolorosa*.

When we contemplate Christ's suffering, we are, more than anywhere else, elevated above historical thinking. Any ordinary historical fact usually has a certain value for those living at the time, but the weight of the event diminishes in importance as the event fades from memory. Nobody will deny that Julius Caesar's conquering of Western Europe was of great historical importance, that it dominated world history of that time in numerous ways. We could even say that we experience the effects and conditions of that conquest in our own time, many centuries later. At the same time, it is also true that the consequences of the conquest of Gallia and Germania and their inclusion in the Roman Empire, which happened some two thousand years ago, have gradually lost their significance. Every historical event has an immediate impact and significant influence the moment it takes place, but its memory fades and its effect weakens as the years go by and new occurrences crowd them out.

All of this is completely different in the case of Golgotha. The Gospels and the other books in the New Testament make it abundantly clear that this one historical fact has value for eternity. This single event caused a fundamental change in the makeup of humanity: it opened the way for millions to obtain eternal redemption, and it liberated untold millions of humans living in different countries and throughout all ages. This single event changed the basic structure of the world; Golgotha radically altered the makeup of a world lying under condemnation and subject to vanity. Now Adam is no longer the exile, the man who roamed the periphery of paradise and was banished from it for eternity. Thanks to Golgotha, Adam has undergone a radical change. The potential for our lives and the totality of our existence have, in principle, been fundamentally altered because of Golgotha. That's why the cross stands in the midst of history as a strange phenomenon. We simply cannot equate an event such as a Roman legion's conquering a city in northern Africa or a Chinese emperor's suppressing a revolt somewhere with the death of Jesus Christ on the cross during that same year. The reason this is impossible is that those three historical events do not run parallel — are not in the same category. The first two are historical facts — no more, no less; the latter has consequences for eternity. The fact is that Golgotha has made it possible that the sun comes up and goes down, that our hearts still beat, that each year the radiant spring spreads a treasure of riches and promise over the world, that hope still vibrates through creation. This is an event without an expiration date: it is eternal in its significance.

It is this instance of immense suffering that deserves our special attention. By now we are well aware that Golgotha is closely connected to the *Urzeit*, the time when certain events took place that dominate human life from the time of Adam until this very moment. It was in that misty *Urzeit* that Adam, created in God's image, fell away from before God's face, was expelled from the Garden of Eden, and was removed far from the Tree of Life. From that unholy moment onward, human beings — each one of us — are exiles in this world, crawling in the dust, so to speak, yet still having in us a secret longing for the Tree of Life. The *Urzeit* determines history; there we find the origins that determine all world events. Because all this is so fundamentally connected to these eternal matters, this is also the reason why the Second Adam had to suffer so greatly. Again we return to Eden, again we listen to God's voice, and again we see how Adam is summoned before the throne. In the distance we faintly detect something of the bright splendor of the cherubim that guard the entrance of the garden. Gethsemane reminds us of that garden of many centuries ago, the garden where death engulfed our race.

When we pay close attention to the arrest of Jesus, we cannot help but notice that there are many small details that are directly connected to what happened in Eden. Anybody who takes the time to read Genesis 3:8-13, and after that meditates on the first verses of John 18, cannot escape the impression that these two Scripture passages complement each other and are directly related. Genesis 3 tells us about a grove, a garden, and so does John 18, this one situated at the foot of the Mount of Olives. Adam hears God's voice in the cool evening hours; Jesus has his immense struggle in Gethsemane during the nighttime hours. The first Adam and the second Adam meet there.

Yet there are also profound differences between these two. The first Adam is still in paradise, standing as yet before the curse; but in the depth of his heart the anxiety already dwells, the unspeakable fearfulness for what is to come. He still wears his crown but does so with fear and trembling. The second Adam stands there in the garden in that dark hour as one cursed, as an exile, as one driven from paradise. He is disfigured — without stature or glory. He is exactly where the first Adam arrived because of his sin. But in the heart of the second Adam is the surrender, the willingness, the deep and complete submission to God's will.

Two moments are pictured here for us, two instances that belong together, two events full of moving similarity and yet of unbridgeable contrast. It is on these two features that Scripture sheds a clear light.

Adam, Where Are You?

"Then the man and his wife heard the sound of the Lord as he walked in the garden in the cool of the day, and they hid from the Lord God among the trees of the garden. But the Lord God called to the man, 'Where are you?'" (Gen. 3:8, 9). Jesus, knowing everything that was going to happen to him, stepped forward and said to them: "Who is it you want?" They answered him: "Jesus of Nazareth." He said to them: "I am he" (John 18:4-5).

These few verses forcefully express the immense contrast between the first Adam and the second Adam, between Eden and Gethsemane. In

Eden the evening breeze whispers through the trees, and Adam recognizes the footsteps of the Lord of the entire earth, who calls him to account. Adam flees from the latter's face and hides among the trees. With Jesus it's the opposite: we see him standing there, as people are calling for him. He stands there as God's Son who has come into the world, as the Word become flesh who has lived among us as the tabernacle of God. He is the expressed image of God's independence. He, the Son of God, is likewise in the garden, but this time it is the human race that is looking for him. In the total stillness of the night, with the silver light of the moon causing the trees to project whimsical shapes, Jesus hears the threatening sound of approaching footsteps in the distance and sees the fluttering light of lanterns and torches shining through the trees. He knows that all of us, as members of the human race, have come to bring him to justice and have him sentenced.

It is clear that we are here confronted with two facts that are diametrically opposed. Adam, the human, is summoned by God: "Adam, where are you?" In Gethsemane the opposite happens: God himself, the Son of God, is summoned by the insolent and blasphemous humans, "God, where are you?" In Eden judgment will come down on Adam and the human race, on all of us, because we have left the way to God, overcome by our desire to be equal to God. In Gethsemane it is God's Son who, "being in the very nature of God did not consider equality with God something to be grasped, but made himself nothing, taking the very nature of a servant, being made in human likeness" (Phil. 2:6-7). It is this Son, in the form of a servant, who is summoned before the judgment seat of humanity, humans who want to judge *him*. Soon after this they will tell him that they do not want such a God, that they cannot peacefully live with such a God, that such a God must be killed. Those terrible verses, found in John 18, are the direct opposite of what was described in Genesis. We, the human race, have made ourselves equal to God, have taken life into our own hands, and we live and feel and act according to the norms of our own understanding. We humans have become a law unto ourselves, and we have refused to heed other laws. And that *adam*, personifying the human race, now submits in Gethsemane to the unfathomable possibility, the absurd chance to take revenge for what at one time took place in Eden. Humans can now stride godlike through the darkness of the garden and exclaim with horrible hubris and boundless brutality: "God, where are you?" Here and now they are able to drag the second Adam before the judgment seat. Here and now they can tie him up with ropes, treating him as a murderer. They can make him a laughingstock and spit on him. Between John 18 and Genesis 3 there is an abyss so immeasurably deep that it makes us shudder.

Yet we can read this same happening in a completely different light. That is the mystery of the *via dolorosa:* that all instances can be understood in a dual sense. We can reverse the entire scene, and it is true even then. The case in both instances is that God is convicted by human judges; at the same time, it is also true that these same human judges are being judged by God. The image can be reversed, put upside down, as it were, and each time it still gives a true picture, still expresses a profound thought. That is the thoroughly mysterious structure of the passion story.

It is also true, after all, that we can read it in such a way that Adam, in Gethsemane, is once again called by God: "Adam, where are you?" Those soldiers who are coming closer and closer, armed with swords and sticks, are instruments of God's will, are in the service of the rulers and thus act in God's name. And yes, God himself acts through them. Jesus confessed this himself in complete surrender: "Shall I not drink the cup that the Father [not humanity, not the soldiers] has given me?" (John 18:11). Jesus, who in this dark hour is being sought by these men, is actually none other than Adam, the original human. He has taken the place where Adam once stood. He has taken upon himself Adam's curse. He has become one with our sin and our plight. And this very same Adam, for the second time, is sought here by God and summoned before his court: "Adam, where are you?"

The first sentence, the sentence in Eden, was only a preliminary one, because it still contained a degree of mercy and still had a hidden promise. Here in Gethsemane all matters approach their final denouement: here comes the ultimate verdict, a judgment without any promise and without any mercy; here is written in indelible letters that humans, who have committed these things, must undergo death in its ultimate sense, in the utterly terrible sense Scripture attaches to it.

When we take a closer look at the particulars of what took place in Gethsemane, a few small contrasts become evident. The first Adam slinks away, hides himself from God's face, and tries to escape judgment when he is called by God. However, Jesus Christ steps forward of his own free will: "Jesus, knowing all that was going to happen to him, stepped forward." There's no question of hiding, no question of trying to escape judgment, no question of trying to avoid the consequences connected to sinful actions. The second Adam steps forward with that miraculous willingness to submit that he had acquired in those painful hours of prayer and struggle. The book of Hebrews expresses it so succinctly: "He learned obedience from what he suffered" (Heb. 5:8).

From all this we can learn much, because Adam's action applies to all people. Sin is never anything other than a flagrant attempt to outrun the consequences of sin. Each one of us, from the very start of history, has harbored the ineradicable desire, on the one hand, to eat from the Tree of Knowledge of Good and Evil but, on the other, to try anxiously to avoid all the terrible consequences that result from this act. We want to be God: we want to direct our own lives, arranging them according to our own ideas; yet we also want to avoid the consequence of sin, which is death. We want to have our cake and eat it, too. We want to taste evil, to greedily drink from the sources of sensual lust, egoism, overweening pride, and deceit; but we also want to be safeguarded from all the terrible effects of those sins. In every one of us there is a desire to hide among the trees of the garden and shy away from death's root cause. That seemingly insignificant act by Adam has eternal repercussions: it is the act of *adam*, of the human in every human being. Even now *adam* is hiding, and even now he hears God's voice, calling him: "Adam, where are you?" When we read Genesis 3, we must always remember that this chapter shows us something that continues to occur, something that keeps on happening in us throughout our entire lives. We can express this in even stronger terms: the entire history of the world, our total human culture, is nothing other than one awe-inspiring attempt to reinstitute a new paradise on the basis of sin, on the foundation of equality with God, a paradise without the cherubim. All those historic struggles to establish a world empire, to base a city of man on the communal will to escape the consequences of sin, are nothing other than crawling away from God.

Human history is, in its deepest sense, rebuilding the Tower of Babel, yet each time the venture is rudely interrupted by the cry to reconsider: "Adam, where are you?" God has addressed fallen humanity ad infinitum, even as it is exiled and cursed by wars and natural disasters. Adam's one act of hiding from the consequence of what he had done lies at the bottom of every sin. He is still hiding among the trees of the garden. Only when we acknowledge this can we understand that Gethsemane restores our essential humanity. In Gethsemane, Adam steps forward, appearing in person, of his own free will, to receive the sentence. In Gethsemane, Adam's fatal step in Eden is rescinded.

This becomes even more pronounced when we consider that the conversation proceeds altogether differently. In Eden, God takes the initiative: there he calls Adam to show himself. In Gethsemane, Jesus speaks up first and asks his captors: "Whom do you seek?" That is not a matter of arrogance or recklessness; it is simply complete surrender. In Gethsemane there is no echo of "Adam, where are you?" because there the second Adam steps forward before God has called him.

If You Are Looking for Me

"The man, Adam, said: 'The woman you put here with me — she gave me some fruit from the tree and I ate it.' Then the Lord God said to the woman, 'What is this you have done?' The woman said, 'The serpent deceived me and I ate'" (Gen. 3:12-13). "Jesus answered, 'I told you that I am he. If you are looking for me, then let these men go'" (John 18:8).

These words set the stage for a new element in the passion story, a development with clear resonances of what once happened in paradise. When Adam and Eve are called by God and questioned concerning their sin, both deny that they are themselves guilty. Both try to blame someone else; at least, both attempt to minimize their part in the misdeed. For this purpose they resort to the utmost of egotism. Adam does not waste a minute in blaming the woman to whom he is so intimately related. He even implies in his answer that God himself is somewhat to blame for giving him this woman. In other words, human beings use any means possible to rid themselves of blame. Even the love humans feel in their hearts for their neighbor is no obstacle to dumping the blame on each other if there is no alternative. That is the tragic story of how the first human beings shifted their responsibility.

We should not forget that here, too, we are dealing with Adam, with the *adam* in all of us, something that is unalterably part of us. We are not discussing a particular phenomenon that happened once upon a time many years ago but that now no longer occurs. No, what we are dealing with here is something that has always remained real and contemporary: as long as the human race dwells on earth, *adam* is in him, with the same inclination that we have so clearly seen described in Genesis 3. It is the sin in every sin, the evil with which we all struggle every day. Indeed, our own life teaches us that nothing is more difficult than to shoulder the full responsibility for our trespasses. Almost always the human element in our nature tries to dodge guilt and shift the blame on others.

Of course, that can be done in different ways. We can do it impersonally by pointing to the circumstances that caused the unfortunate event. Hidden behind those circumstances lies the higher order that is responsible for everything. We can also couch the blame in personal terms, by pointing the finger at the proverbial neighbor or even at God as the instigator of the sin that we have actually committed. Whatever is the case, in every sin there is an element of blame-denial. What is remarkable in this is that it is based on social cohesion. In our sinning we do not stand isolated from one another: almost every sin we commit happens in community. Numerous sins are inherently of that nature. The sins of adultery and of quarreling and dispute, for example, are communally based. But also those sins that are individually committed still happen in the greater context of society, and society as such has been the provocation behind them. That is the reason why, when a crime is committed, we can hardly make one person totally responsible for the act. Our judicial systems, which as a rule punish an offender in isolation, are always more or less one-sided, because they do not take into account the role played by the parents, teachers, or friends of that person. All sin carries with it a degree of communality, as it finds its roots in society. We do not sin as individuals, but as members of our greater social environment.

It is in that context that we must look at Adam's excuse ("the woman you have given me"), his defense that the society in which the Lord allowed him to be born is to blame. Humanity shifts the responsibility for personal evil onto the greater community of which it forms a part and hides behind his fellow member of society. That is so basic in sin that even small children use this excuse.

Seen in that light, Christ's reply is even more exceptional: "If you are looking for me, let the others go." The context is also relevant here. But in this case, society is not asked to shoulder a person's guilt or responsibility; on the contrary, society is protected from being held responsible for a person's own misstep. The second Adam does not point at the fellow citizens he interacts with, nor to his disciples, to accuse them; on the contrary, he relieves them, lets them hide behind him by taking full responsibility himself. That amounts to turning matters upside down, to reversing the question of guilt. The second Adam assumes the entire burden of sin, and so, by taking on all responsibility, pays the debt for the society in which he is rooted.

In that respect, the word of the Christ is the exact opposite of Adam's words. Both originate in the communal source of sin; that is the scenario in which evil was allowed to flourish. But the other side of the coin is radically different. What happened in Eden finds its remedy in Gethsemane. In Gethsemane one man alone takes upon himself the load of sin of the many and holds a protective hand over all who are his own. The solidarity of sin is worked through in a totally different way in Gethsemane than in Eden.

Surrendering to the Tribunal

"Then the detachment of soldiers with its commander and the Jewish officials arrested Jesus. They bound him and brought him first to Annas" (John 18:12). John ends his description of the events in Gethsemane with a short report on the arrest of Jesus. "They arrested him and bound him." In these simple and sober — yet soul-gripping — words, the Gospel writer tells how Jesus assumed our shame upon himself.

For a moment the thought flashes through our minds that it really is God who is bound by our foul human hands. He is that same God who appeared in this world, who out of the sublime loftiness of his eternal abode came down to us so that we could observe his radiance. He is the same God who confronted us in our overweening pride with the terrible words "Woe to you!" He is the same God who called out to the old covenant people, "O Jerusalem, Jerusalem, you who killed the prophets and stoned those sent to you, how often have I longed to gather your children together, as a hen gathers her chicks under her wings, but you were not willing" (Matt. 23:37). It is the same God who, in his benevolence, stretched out his hands to lost mankind. It is he who is now bound and escorted under guard through the city streets like a murderer. Do we slap God in his face with our own death penalty? Do we play our hideous game with God? Do we really want to say with every sinew of our nature that we do not want such a God who has come to us to purchase us with his life and thus to make us one with him? With cruel hands we grab God ("They arrested him and bound him"), the handcuffed God, the God who can no longer bother us in our everyday affairs, the God who is powerless, repelled, and rejected by this mixed-up world. Here humans want to be king; here they want to play the godless game to the end, without any interruption; here they can brook no interference from above. Amid their celebrations the humans, drunk with sin, do not want to hear the reproachful cry "Adam, where are you?" Humans want to be left alone, alone by themselves, alone with the world that they hold in their greedy hands and on which they have thrown themselves with the eagerness of a thirst that can never be slaked. Here humans in general, frail as we are — "like a drop in the bucket" (Isa. 40:15), like "dust and ashes" — are able to rudely grab God's big and mighty hands and push down God's powerful arms to overpower them and bind them with large ropes. Here we humans — vanity personified — can drag the arrested God along roads of our own choosing to the place we have determined. God in shackles.

When we imagine this for a moment, we shudder. It is as if the gates of hell open up, as if everything is upside down, as if we find ourselves in a world without any sense. But then we realize that this picture is not what it seems, that we are not dealing here with God in shackles but with the man Adam who is bound hand and foot. Once again we are confronted with the mystery of the reversibility that is so typical of the entire passion story, which holds true in two respects: where it points to the shackled God, dragged along on the *via dolorosa* by human hands; but also where it tells us of the shackled Adam who is summoned by God before his tribunal. The passion chronology covers two angles simultaneously: it is the highest possible peak of the flame of sin, the most abhorrent expression of what constitutes the essence of sin; and it is the just sentence of God over all human guilt. These two aspects of the passion story turn it into a stirring drama of scarcely imaginable proportions. At each moment we stand both before the portal of hell and before the gate of heaven.

At any rate, the captive standing here before us is none other than Adam, we humans, with all our eminent gifts and powers, the lords of creation, we who have dared to tear ourselves from God and break away from the majestic harmony of God's kingdom. We, humanity at large, have tried, in our boundless pride, to become equal with God, to become autonomous, to determine the law of life for ourselves. There we stand, the highest but also the most despicable of all creatures, the strongest but also the weakest, the most noble but also the most degenerate. This is Adam, banished from the garden, who as an exile had to flee outside the gates of paradise, and who with all the boundless energy he possessed, threw himself onto the world as his last remaining domain. This is Adam, a hopeless and helpless creature, disillusioned and defeated. To top it all off, God's verdict grabs him, drags him out of the garden, and shackles him, so that he, robbed of his strength, must travel the road of one damned by God. Here his hands are bound, those hands that were so often lifted up to commit shameful acts. Here his mouth is muzzled, that instrument of frequent curses. Here his feet are forced to go where God wants him to go, those feet he has used so frequently and cheerfully to leap on his prey. Here we are, the great and glorious humans, creators of so many cultural treasures, the builders of world-class cities, the designers of palaces, the scientists and poets — always engaged, always at work. But here Adam is deprived of his last resort, his power. Here he collapses and sinks into the abyss of helplessness and misery. What awaits him here is nothing other than the flaming judgment of the divine. It is a terrible thing to fall in the hands of the living God.

This is the finish of all culture. The chisel of the sculptor falls from his hand, the brush of the painter drops to the ground, the builder of world empires sees his dreams evaporate. Here we stand, powerless, as sheep on the verge of slaughter. This is the end of all history. History means always being busy creating, always inventing new forms for the visions of the human mind. History is becoming; it is action. It is a never-ending attempt to erect in this battered world an empire of beauty and harmony. Here I stand, handcuffed, declaring myself equal with God, now driven from God's garden and awaiting the terrible verdict about to be delivered.

And yet this one man, this unique Adam, is himself different. He is the only one whose hands are not soiled, whose feet have not been swift to shed blood (Isa. 59:7), whose throat has not been an open grave (Ps. 5:10). He is the only Adam who was not *adam*, in whom was never found that ingredient that can be called the most essential human trait. This one Adam, the innocent one, who in his unfathomable love has made himself one with our guilt and has taken it upon himself, stands there in the place of the *adam* who is in all of us. He stands in the place of the entire human race. There he is not himself, nor does he live there himself, but he is what we are. He becomes one with us. In him the entire human race, the whole of world history, is facing its inevitable and terrible end. He is "humanity"; he is "the world." He is the demise of all human skill and creativity. He is the shackled *adam*.

CHAPTER 6

The High-Priestly Verdict

The High Priest as Judge

We tend to have a one-sided view of the task of the priests in Israel. We think of their work only as it pertains to the temple service and the ceremonies that form part of the usual worship service. However, in line with the old traditions in Israel, reality was a different thing entirely. The task of the priests was much broader than what we have usually conceived it to be. They were not only engaged in matters of worship, but were also involved with a wide range of medical and juridical matters. It is especially the latter that will be the subject of this chapter.

Of course, the primary task of the priests still was to impress on the people the rules and ordinances God had set out by way of Moses: they had to "teach the Israelites all the decrees the Lord has given them through Moses" (Lev. 10:11). This means that it was the duty of the priests to provide instruction, and they were entrusted to look after the young people so that they would grow up to be good members of church and nation. At the same time they were assigned a judicial role. They knew the law — studied it daily — so that when difficulties arose, they were the best equipped to deal with those problems. That is why, from time immemorial, the judiciary, or at least the appeals process, was completely in the hands of the priests. As a rule, the elders locally would take care of the minor cases, but in the more important disputes, the levitical priests were charged with rendering a verdict (cf. Deut. 17:8-9). In subsequent years this often became a matter of dispute between the royalty and the priesthood (according to W. H. Gispen in *Bijbelsch Handboek*). However, the Mosaic law was very clear that the priests had a special responsibility in connection with judicial cases. Of course, this was particularly true when it had to do with religious matters in a more direct sense; but since all matters were prescribed by God in Israel, the boundaries here were always difficult to distinguish, because church was synonymous with nation in Israel. The law applied to life in all its manifestations and determined the order for everything as stipulated by God. Every action, of whatever nature, applied to both the nation and the church. Every trespass was not only committed against the people, but also was a sin within the context of the church. That is why religious life as such touched on a very wide range of applications, and the reason why the church, because of the ordinances instituted by God, had to oversee the correct way of life.

So it is quite natural that Jesus, after having been handcuffed by the soldiers, is brought to the residence of the high priest to be judged there. In Jesus' day the court proceedings were handled by the high priest, together with the so-called Sanhedrin, the council of the elders and notables. In general, this body dealt with offenses concerning religious matters, and that included those having to do with the Temple service.

The Court Proceedings

We now enter the meeting room of the Sanhedrin and observe the proceedings there in more detail. We will not analyze the preliminary investigation by Annas, because that involves some difficulties for which we do not, as yet, have a solution. What the Sanhedrin is doing is more important. The Gospels point out that the first accusation, having to do with the Temple, had received sufficient support for further action. Jesus, according to some witnesses, was supposed to have said that he could demolish the Temple and rebuild it in three days (Matt. 26:61). The Gospel of Mark phrases the complaint somewhat differently: it says that Jesus was accused not only of having declared that he could break down the Temple, but that also of claiming that he would, in fact, do so, and after that would build another Temple in three days, one not made with human hands. But, Mark adds, these accusations were at cross-purposes (Mark 14:57-59); in any case, they are at odds with what Jesus really had said (see John 2:19).

The initial accusation was that Jesus had defamed the Temple. The Jews considered the Temple and everything associated with it holy, and any defamation of it was considered cursing God's holiness and was severely punished. The buying and selling going on in the outer court was really contrary to this Temple veneration, but greed proved to be the more powerful motivation in this instance, even though they did believe that sacrilege against the temple meant profaning God, who is worshiped in the Temple. It is truly remarkable that the indictment initially was fixated on this question. It is undoubtedly there so that we may see God's providence at work here. God does not want to see Jesus judged on the basis of some trivial charges and side issues; God wants Jesus to be accused of the most radical and central indictment possible, that he had desecrated the Temple, had spoken about it in demeaning and flippant ways. With that he has shown that he despises the service of Yahweh and has placed himself outside the communion of the church.

We must remember that the Temple was paradise, the ever-eternal in this temporal world. The Temple stood outside history. Of course, these Temple buildings have had their own history of being destroyed and rebuilt, and in ages past the Temple had been a mere tent. But those were mere external appearances because the idea of the Temple was eternal, unalterable. One world-shaking event would follow another in frantic succession, and wars and natural disasters would slay their millions; but there, high above us, fixed for eternity, in the middle of the world in flames, stood the Temple, the last memory of the lost paradise. Once a year the high priest, Adam, was allowed to spend a few moments there, standing again before the Tree of Life and before the face of God, who had created heaven and earth. There Adam, as exiled humanity, was allowed to enter carrying the blood of sacrifice in his hands. The high priest was permitted to linger a short while there, where he would see the pensive cherubim, now without the flaming sword, gaze in holy amazement at the cover of the ark, the mercy seat, which symbolized the infinite mystery of redemption. That was the Temple, the only place in this rudderless world where peace prevailed, where there still was life, where God lived among his people. And Jesus was accused of having defiled this Temple, of having derided paradise. He was accused of having said, in his boundless pride, that he would break down the Temple and build another one. He had ridiculed God's paradise on earth and had said that he himself could create a new paradise. That was his sin.

And was that not really the original sin, the *adam* in all of us? Have we not always, throughout the ages, been busy at breaking down the Temple, breaking down paradise, and attempting via our own culture, our own art and science, our own music and film, to build a new paradise? Isn't that the sin in all sin? Has Adam ever done anything other than what Jesus has done here? Has Adam not turned his back on paradise? Has he not despised communion with God? And has he not, godlike, wanted to build a new paradise? And was that not the reason he was driven out of the Garden of Eden, far away from the Tree of Life?

Indeed, Jesus is Adam; his sin is Adam's sin. God does not want Jesus to be accused of any other wrongdoing than the accusation brought against Adam. The accusation was that he had vilified God's dwelling among people and in cold-blooded arrogance had pretended to build his own paradise. World history must return to the point of departure. Adam is judged because he once denied God's glory; Jesus is now accused of what Adam has done wrong. Here world history momentarily holds its breath; time stands still, and no date marks this event, because it harks back to what happened in the *Urzeit*. Everything reverts to its point of departure. "That's what you have done, Adam! You have sold paradise down the river; you have despised the life in which you breathe, in which you could enjoy communion with God and hear his voice in the soft evening breeze; you have not respected the Tree of Life and the throne of the Almighty. You have even dared to vilify all this in your fatal pride, thinking that you could find life and shalom outside of God. Here God's accusation rebounds on you, here God is calling you to account. You, Adam, have destroyed paradise, you have broken down the Temple, in the fateful illusion that you are powerful enough to erect a new Temple."

The Charge by the High Priest

And yet it was not God's will that Jesus would ultimately be sentenced on the accusation of the Temple issue. "Many testified falsely against him, but their statements did not agree," writes Mark. The accusation, however serious, was after all declared inadmissible because no two witnesses could be found who completely agreed with each other. God himself steered this process from beginning to end because he, in his good pleasure, wished that Jesus would be sentenced on the grounds of the most serious and the most grievous accusation ever brought against a person, the accusation of self-deification.

"'You will not surely die,' the serpent said to the woman, 'For God knows that when you eat of it your eyes will be opened, and you will be like God, knowing good and evil'" (Gen. 3:4-5).

You will be like God!

"And the high priest said to him, 'I charge you under oath by the living God, tell us if you are the Christ, the Son of God.'"

'Yes, it is as you say,' Jesus replied. Then the high priest tore his clothes and said, 'He has spoken blasphemy! Why do we need any more witnesses?'" (Matt. 26:63-65). Jesus was sentenced because he made himself equal to God.

When we compare these two texts, we must realize that all sin inherently has two aspects. Sin contains what we may call a priestly part: that involves self-deification, the act of pushing God out of our lives and thus breaking ourselves loose from communion with God. Sin is severing the tie with God, an escape from the Holy One. Besides that, sin also has a royal aspect: it severs us from a meaningful connection to God's kingdom. Humanity at large has posited its own will and its own desire over against the all-penetrating and all-fulfilling will of the Creator. In other words, the priestly side of sin applies to our ontic status as human beings. In that status, even as we exist in God and through God, we seek a place to stand outside God. The royal side of sin, on the other hand, touches on our capacity to exercise free will, and thus it affects the moral order of the world. And behind these two stands the prophetic aspect, which has caused us to refuse truth and refuse to remain in the truth (John 8:44). The high priest accuses Jesus of the great priestly sin, of tearing loose from communion with God, of self-deification.

We really cannot fathom these matters without being touched by several soul-shaking notions. We must see Caiaphas here as humanity, as Adam, as representative of the human race. He stands across from Jesus, who was named God's Son. There Jesus stands, the one who had descended from heaven to earth to accomplish, as a humble servant, the work the Father had asked him to do. There Jesus stands, the one who had voluntarily emptied himself of the eternal glory of the divine magnificence because he had not considered "being equal with God" something to be grasped. There Jesus stands, the one who is the only person who did not make himself equal to God, who did not — not even for a moment — sever intimate contact with God. On the contrary, even though he was God, he lived fully as human on earth and there brought God's word.

Facing him is Adam, Caiaphas, humanity as such, who did place God's crown on his own head, who, out of a deep desire to be God, alienated himself from God and assumed a different posture, far outside the light of the eternal. And this same Caiaphas, the man who had elevated himself to the status of God, throws the terrible accusation at the real Son of God: that he had blasphemed God in his delusional desire to be equal to God. Here we encounter the greatest untruth in world history. Adam accuses God of calling himself God. Adam drags God before the judgment seat and tells him to his face that he is totally wrong in calling himself God. Here humanity — you and I — unjustifiably violate the image of the unseen, the eternal, the only-wise God. In other words, Caiaphas is the high priest, and he has often entered into the Holy of Holies. There he has stood in the innermost Holy Place, where, according to the ancient tradition, the cherubim reside, without their flaming swords, their faces looking down on the mystery of redemption. In all of this Caiaphas has been a prototype of, and has foreshadowed, the great high priest, the true Adam, the one who one day would enter the true Holy Place to bring about eternal redemption. This Caiaphas is himself a forerunner, an image of Christ; in this unholy moment, Caiaphas, this forerunner and prototype of Christ, faces the true reality and fulfillment of what he is in his deepest essence. And here the model pretends to portray flesh and blood; the shadow pretends to be the real thing; the symbol pretends to represent what it symbolizes.

It can also be phrased another way: Christ is the focal point, the deepest meaning of Israel's priesthood. Without Christ the Old Testament priesthood is an empty and meaningless ceremony. The Christ of God is the ultimate reason for the existence of Caiaphas, the central focus of his office. In this moment, Caiaphas attacks the very person in whom he himself finds his meaning, for whose sake he exists, whose life and works he is supposed to exemplify. Here the high priest does away with the very meaning of his own life, denies exactly what he, in his life's ultimate sense, is. We can penetrate still deeper into the enigmatic event taking place in the palace of Caiaphas, who represents the ancient traditions of the people of Israel. Throughout Israel's history, through the course of many centuries, its people had strongly and fervently longed for a Redeemer who would come one day. Jacob, on his deathbed, had prophesied of his coming. David had expressed his greatness in moving songs. Isaiah and Jeremiah, Micah and Ezekiel had foreseen his glory. Israel's very existence was centered on the coming Messiah; that was its raison d'être, the sole purpose for which it was in the world. Think of Israel apart from the Messiah, and its status is reduced to the level of an ordinary people, like any other nation. The Messiah was the ultimate meaning of Israel's nationhood.

And here's what happens: in this disturbing moment, Caiaphas, who represents Israel, dares to accuse the Christ of God of self-deification. In this same moment, Israel attacks exactly that for which it has longed throughout its long existence, about which it has prophesied, and to which it has been a witness among the nations. Jacob, who had looked for God's deliverance (Gen. 49:18), discards this salvation as worthless at the very moment it finally arrives. The trunk denies the shoot sprouted from it (Isa. 11:1), Jacob renounces the star that will come out of him (Num. 24:17). The hope of the fathers was cruelly cut down. From generation to generation, Israel has longed for — indeed, pined after — the eventual coming of the one who would, at one time, bring salvation. The prophets have testified that this great Redeemer would be none other than God himself, the Son of God who is to come into the world. And now that this great son of David, this Messiah, has finally arrived in the world, he is labeled a blasphemer by that same Israel, a person who has made himself equal to God. Has there ever been anything as tragic as this denial?

And why could Caiaphas, with the unanimous approval of the Sanhedrin, accuse Jesus of this crime? Why did none of these men recognize in Jesus the Messiah promised by God? They had occupied their time by studying the scriptures, and they knew all the prophecies that spoke about the coming Savior by heart. Why was it that none of them recognized Jesus? Why was it that none of them were struck by the great similarity between this rabbi from Nazareth and the long-expected one who was anointed of God? How was it possible that none of these men, not a single member of official Israel, had noticed the splendor of God's majesty in the humble figure of the suffering "servant of the Lord"? What blinded all these men to the extent that they could not detect the hidden halo on the head of this king sent by God?

The ultimate reason must have been that they no longer knew God, and that is why they could not recognize Jesus. Jesus had all God's features in his being, in all his works, but they had no eye for it. The Israel of Jesus' day carried a different image of God; it dreamed about a different God from the God visible to the world in Jesus Christ. Israel was a religious nation: it would never miss going to the Temple to call on Yahweh in his sanctuary. But they understood something quite different when they used the name Yahweh. They had their own God, one conforming to their own ideas. They had a self-invented God whom they honored in the Temple, for whom they offered sacrifices, and to whom they sang their hymns of praise. They had become estranged from the hand of God and had slowly but surely forgotten his image. Then they had started to fashion a God after the formulation of their own heart and according to their own image, a God more in line with their own conception and ideas. He was nothing but a formidable projection of what they were themselves: unpredictable, belligerent, cruel, opinionated, and narrow-minded. Their god was just like what they were. They had adored that new God and served him, and they had not understood that serving him was the same as serving themselves, that giving him the glory meant that they gloried in their own accomplishments. They had lived inside that dream of a new God, and in their hearts they jealously guarded that new image, embroidered as it was with Bible texts. They had deformed and twisted the Old Testament to such an extent that it conformed to the God they had chosen for themselves.

When Jesus appeared on the scene, as the image of the true God, when he had explained to them and shown in their midst who God really was, they did not recognize him. They then exclaimed, "This is not God, not the God we know and have chosen." They "did not know his voice" (John 10:4), and they did not hear him "because they did not belong to God" (John 8:47). They found Jesus' words strange: he spoke to them about a different

Yahweh, one they did not believe in and for whom they felt no love. That is why, in the name of their own God, they were now judging Jesus, speaking judgment over the one true God, over God himself. In essence they were saying: "You are not God, and we do not know you; you claim honor for yourself that is not yours." In the name of the God of their dreams they sentence the true God, claiming that he is not God, because they do not know him, asserting that he claims unwarranted honor. They shout back at him that their God is different from the humble figure portrayed by Jesus, that they do not recognize in the Son of man God's majestic glory, on which they have banked their hope.

That is the real basis of the dramatic event taking place in the high priest's palace. The apostle John has most acutely understood the true dimension of the dialogue between Jesus and Israel, and in his Gospel he reveals the fundamental facts. Jesus is "the Truth" (John 14:6); whoever has seen him "has seen the Father" (John 14:9); Jesus is "the Word" that proclaims to the world who God is (John 1:14). When Caiaphas, speaking on behalf of Israel, accuses Jesus of blasphemy, he does so in the name of the imagined God that Israel in its unclean imagination had invented. But they did not want the God who had turned his face to the world in Jesus Christ. They had no delight in him.

In Jesus Christ we are faced once again with the terrible reality that everything that has transpired in this suffering saga is the flip side of what once took place in the Garden of Eden. There God said to Adam and Eve (and to us as the human race), "Because you have made yourself to be a god and have cast me from the throne, that is why you will die." Here, in the palace of Caiaphas, Adam says to God: "Because you have made yourself God, and have cast me from the throne, that is why you must die." Oh, we remained religious, we kept on honoring gods, gods of our own making, and we did not want to admit that all this God-veneration was ultimately nothing but secretive self-adulation, that all our love for God was nothing but a clandestine love affair with self, that all our divine service was but a flimsy form of self-service. Now, borne up by the notion that he himself is God, that God is like him, Caiaphas (the human) summons the only true God before *his* judgment seat and says to *him*: "You are not allowed to be who you are; we do not want you the way you are; we can only know you when you become as we are. You have blasphemed God:

that is, you, a mere mortal, have blasphemed me; you have blasphemed the God whom we have formed after our image and likeness. That is why you deserve death."

When we pursue this to the end, we shake our heads in utter dismay. Here hell is opened wide, and everything is turned upside down: earth pronounces judgment on heaven; the creature dares to convict the Creator, who is to be praised forever, Everything is out of kilter, and we are exposed to utter madness. Through all this resonates the mocking laugh from hell, where a feeling of demonic delight vibrates. Here the universe holds its breath, and the pillars of the earth shake. Here we approach an unfathomable abyss. For a moment the scary thought flashes through our mind that suddenly, overwhelmed by this utterly mad *danse macabre*, this horrible world would sink away into nothingness. This moment is the most terrible, the most perilous hour in the entire history of the world.

The Lamb That Is Slain

Yet here, too, we encounter the mysterious reversibility already noted above. Everything that has happened during Christ's suffering is true in a double sense: it all has a dual function. The greatest enigma of the suffering event is that it is both the zenith of sin and the heart of grace.

Caiaphas, after all, speaks here in his priestly dignity. He is not just a random person; rather, he is God's high priest, endowed by God with a sacred office. And it is in his priestly capacity that he lays violent hands on the only true sacrificial lamb. And the man in front of him is none other than Adam, who has covenanted himself to the entire human race. He has entered our nature, has made our debt his. It is he about whom God at one time has said, "When you eat of it you will surely die" (Gen. 2:17). It is he who, with head bowed, was banned from Eden, awaiting the definitive judgment that was to come one day. It is he who was burdened with the curse of the entire human race. It is about him that the high priest, in the name of God, says, "See, you have heard his blasphemy; he deserves the death penalty."

Caiaphas represents here the culmination of the entire Old Testament priesthood, the last of a long line of high priests who have for centuries of-

The High-Priestly Verdict

fered sacrifices for sin. In Caiaphas the Old Testament priesthood obtains its full reality and reaches its summit. All earlier high priests foreshadowed him. Only Caiaphas is the real one, only he has to deal with the true sacrificial Lamb, with the true Adam. If Caiaphas had only had an inkling who it was who stood before him as the sacrificial Lamb, he would not have dared to offer the innocent Lamb of God. He would have backed out in total dismay, and he would have cried out, "I need to be sentenced by you!" But now he is blind and has no notion of what is about to happen. Being completely devoid of insight, as one who understands nothing and fails to grasp what is really happening, this clueless high priest, the last of a long line, places his stained hands on the pure, the perfect, and spotless sacrificial lamb that bears the sin of the world.

Not for a moment do the words that Isaiah prophesied dawn on Caiaphas: "He was oppressed and afflicted, yet he did not open his mouth; he was led like a lamb to the slaughter, and as a sheep before her shearers is silent, so he did not open his mouth" (Isa. 53:7). And yet this entire prophecy was intimately related to what he was doing at that very moment — as these words directly applied to him. He acted as though he were a sleepwalker, but what he did was the greatest and most decisive act in the entire history of the world.

God himself did this through Caiaphas, the high priest he had anointed. It was God who, having chosen this holy and sacrificial lamb, had taken it and prepared it for death. Through Caiaphas and his words, God's holy voice sounded, and through him God pronounced his judgment on Adam. God himself blindfolded this vain high priest so that he, as one unable to see, would act in this way in order to do "what your power and will had decided beforehand should happen" (Acts 4:28).

Contemplating these things to the very bottom, our hearts become heavy. What is the life of the human being if such things can happen to him? God's majestic, sweeping action operates through the blinded and besotted deed of the self-important human. Caiaphas does what he does willy-nilly; or perhaps it is God doing in him and through him what he, even remotely, cannot suspect. God, in Caiaphas, returns to paradise and pronounces divine damnation over Adam, who had made himself equal to God. Everything in this event is different from what it appears to be. Caiaphas, the lost soul who has also lost his mind, stands here in God's place; Jesus, God's son, stands here in the place of humanity. Caiaphas, whose every thought is sinful, and who is unworthy of his priestly office in every respect, acts here as the judge; Jesus, the sinless Son of God, stands here as the offender, the one burdened with sin. And operating throughout this dialogue between Caiaphas and Jesus are God's mighty works, unseen and unfathomable by even a single person. Caiaphas acts on behalf of God, pronouncing sentence in God's name; but what he does, at the same time, is the biggest sin possible, the lowest point in his fall from God. Here something mysteriously divine takes place, something that we are included in as links, but that, in its essence, goes far beyond our imagination, so that none of us can really comprehend this. The high priest offers the Lamb of God that takes away the sin of the world as sacrifice, and he does not know that this is God's Lamb. He is motivated by jealousy, hubris, and blindness, and yet his deed is the most critical deed of any that humanity has ever done.

At the precise instant that Caiaphas pronounces Jesus' death sentence, the high priest's function is terminated. The Old Testament office has now lost its meaning: when Caiaphas sends this sacrificial Lamb away for slaughter, something that throughout the centuries had so often been foreshadowed by generations of high priests, his task is finished, his office then and there forever ended. In the future, the high priest may solemnly continue to enter the Holy of Holies year after year; but that ceremonial act is now useless, makes no more sense. Caiaphas, by this single act, has forever nullified the high-priestly ritual. The very Temple, that marvelous structure with its rich symbolism, has become superfluous. It still stands there on Mount Zion, but now it is a mere heap of stones — without meaning and purpose. Caiaphas's act has dissolved the Temple. A few hours before, Jesus had been accused of saying that he would destroy the Temple; but Caiaphas is the one who has actually done so, and he is surely unable to rebuild it in three days. Caiaphas's act finalizes the entire Old Testament priestly service: it is the last act performed by the priest of the old covenant. When we see that in its proper perspective, it strikes us that it is both the most horrible and the most magnificent of all actions performed by the former priesthood. Here the liturgical function of the priest shows that the priesthood has not only become a sham, but also that it has reached its fulfillment.

However, our attention should cease to be fixated on the priest, and should rather be focused on the lamb, the Lamb of God that dominates this entire history. In Old Testament worship, the lamb had no inkling of what was involved; only the priest knew. The lamb was blind, but the priest knew the meaning of the lamb. In the enormous reality of the New Testament, the priest is blind, and only the Lamb knows what is happening. The priest acts, but he does not know what his act entails; the Lamb suffers and knows exactly why he suffers.

We could phrase it differently: the Lamb himself is the true high priest, the one after the order of Melchizedek. Caiaphas is a mere phantom, because the true high priest is Jesus himself. The dialogue between Caiaphas and Jesus is in its deepest sense a dialogue between the high priest and the Lamb in Christ himself. Christ himself consecrates his own body, offers himself for the sins of the world. In the final analysis, there is, in Caiaphas's palace, in the night of all nights, only one person, the one and only eternal high priest, who pronounces his death sentence by himself and over himself. Here is the one who offers himself as a sacrificial lamb in order to save the world. All the rest is illusion and of no consequence; only this is essential. The only veritable high priest is the second Adam, the really true human. With his own blood, through his own blood, and via his own death, he enters paradise and approaches God's throne, taking with him all those who belong to him as his eternal, inalienable possession. That is something the cherubim had never suspected; that is why their eyes look down in utter amazement on the cover of the Ark of the Covenant. God's foolishness is wiser than man's wisdom. "What no eye has seen, no ear has heard, no mind has conceived" — that is what God has prepared "for those who love him" (1 Cor. 2:9).

CHAPTER 7

"I Don't Know the Man"

The Disciples

It is truly remarkable that throughout the passion story the Gospel writers weave a strand of a particular color and character. The connecting element is the attitude of the disciples. In addition to the priestly aspect before Caiaphas and the royal aspect before Pontius Pilate, the conduct of the disciples could be called the *third motif* that dominates the passion story.

To some degree the disciples find themselves outside the real goings-on: they play no role in the verdict to be pronounced over the Son of man; they have no seat in the Sanhedrin; they do not participate in the jeering of the excited crowd before Pilate's court that ended in the passionate cry "Crucify him, crucify him!" Thus they bear no direct responsibility for Jesus' death. Only one of them, Judas, plays a direct role in the story: John's Gospel mentions that Judas was among those who arrested Jesus (John 18:5). He had abandoned his place among the circle of disciples and had gone over to those who were the enemies of the Christ of God. All the others were more or less passive bystanders in the trial and conviction of their master.

Nevertheless, the disciples occupied a significant place in the totality of the passion drama. They were the first to hear the message of the suffering that was to come, and their reaction was one of vehement denial. Time and again they turned away in disbelief when Jesus wanted to share with them the inevitable events of his death and resurrection. They utterly refused to entertain this reality. They so closed their minds to this possibility that Luke, in exasperation, writes: "The disciples did not understand any of this. Its meaning was hidden from them and they did not know what he was talking about" (Luke 18:34). They had their own ideas about what should happen to Jesus and what Jesus should do, and that scenario had no place for the raw reality of the cross. They went along, as unsuspecting children, with Jesus on the dark road that ended in death. When the night of terror finally began to descend on Jesus, they not only failed to assist or comfort him in any way, but, on the contrary, repeatedly caused extra difficulties for him. In Gethsemane, in that frightful hour of surrender to God's will, they were found sleeping. When the soldiers approached to apprehend Jesus, the disciples started to fight back in reckless indignation, taking the risk that at any moment this quiet, nocturnal garden could turn into a horrendous murder scene.

No, the disciples just didn't get it. They really had no role to play in the larger scheme of the suffering Christ because, in their reluctance and stupidity, they repeatedly made highly questionable choices. In the later phases of their master's suffering, they abandoned him completely and vanished into the background — not to be heard from again. Indeed, the disciples, intimately connected as they were with the most astounding event ever — something that literally took place before their eyes — did not seem to realize it at all. Their preconceptions blinded them. These hours, the most dramatic in world history, passed them by unnoticed.

In all this we must see the disciples as acting in unison. There were lots of differences among them: variations in talent and temperament, some with more and some with less understanding and insight. But on one point there were no differences: they acted as one man. As so often before that night, it was again Peter who became their spokesman. His impulsive and spontaneous persona was often particularly prone to do something exceedingly rash or to express himself in vehement terms, fired up by his deeply emotional nature. But whatever Peter said and did, it is fully in line with what all of them felt deep down. They all would have done or said the same thing if they had had the courage to express themselves in that way. Throughout the passion story the disciples act collectively, one in feelings and of one mind.

I will not elaborate further on the many other elements present in the heartbreaking experience of the disciples as they traveled down this path of immense suffering. However, there is one event to which the Gospels devote extra special attention, and that is Peter's denial. That matter is described in great detail and relayed to us with all the particulars. If we want to understand Christ's suffering, we must deal with this event.

Not Known

From a psychological point of view, it is not difficult to grasp how it happened that Peter lost his mind when he denied knowing the Lord three times in Caiaphas's residence. As a simple fisherman from the countryside of Galilee, he felt small and nervous in these upper-class surroundings, where servants walked around with refreshments, and grandeur and luxury were evident in multiple ways. The terrible strain of these last few days, and the indescribable disappointment that had overpowered Peter in Gethsemane when Jesus allowed himself to be taken without any resistance, had stifled all calm reflection and had brought on a state of bewilderment and despair. His overwrought mind was plagued with nightmares, a natural reaction to his rash conduct in Gethsemane. Behind each door he suspected an enemy; in every footstep he heard somebody who wanted to attack him. In this irritable frame of mind he felt like he was surrounded by lurking enemies. We can easily understand all this, and it is of some interest accounting for it.

And yet, when we further consider Peter's act of denial, we must not forget that we are dealing with factors other than the kind of reaction that can be explained by psychology. We are dealing with the darkest of all dark nights here, the night in which the verdict is reached concerning the very existence of the universe, concerning God's entire immense world, with all its suns and planets and infinite depths. The crux of the matter here is whether the world, already subjected to rape and curse, will sink away into inevitable annihilation, or will instead escape and emerge saved and reborn. Here we have entered the most critical hour in the history of the world, the most perilous moment since that horrible hour in Eden when God's judgment was pronounced over us and our world. Nothing in this hour happens by chance: there is no room here for offhand remarks, arbitrary words welling up from the heart of one person, from a man caught in very special circumstance. Everything spoken here is of the utmost significance, and all centuries converge here. This brief hour will express whatever the human mind has ever contemplated and whatever God's wise counsel has thought about the human race. Here all boundaries of time and space have been eliminated; here we stand in the center of infinity; here the most profound realities of life and mind are exposed; here all that stands by itself and happens by chance disappears; here is no room for moderation and vagueness; here, in the night of all nights, every gesture, every motion, every word has an infinitely exalted meaning. All nations and generations are represented here, and all eras bow down to witness this brief point in time. We, too, stand in the center here, and our lives are also shaken to the core in this immense happening.

Once we have seen this, we also understand that Peter does not appear here as an individual, as a fisherman from Galilee, as a human being in his historical and psychological setting. Everything a person does or says in these grand moments has to do with his human calling: in other words, it is somehow connected to the extratemporal sphere. In the critical moments of human existence, it is not the individual, the ordinary man on the street, who speaks. No, what these circumstances reveal is humans in their humanness — the voice of humanity itself. That always happens when we, in the confusing distractions of our trivial existence, are thrown back on the questions of life, when we are faced with matters of life and death. This was even more true in that singular hour, when the universe held its breath, when it was a question of life and death for us all, when our ultimate redemption was at stake. Peter is not the accidental observer here; he is the spokesman here. He stands in his office, just as he did in Caesarea Philippi, when he confessed Jesus as the Christ, the Son of the living God. Here he speaks with the same authenticity as he did then — on behalf of all disciples. In him and through him the church speaks: it is the church herself that has uttered her word regarding the Son of man in Caiaphas's residence.

Of course, in that fateful hour Peter was not aware of it. He simply felt utterly alone, abandoned, groping and stumbling as one lost in a fog, not knowing where he would end up. He had no clue about the immense importance of what was taking place, nor did he see the role he had to play here. God had his purposes for Peter, something Peter did not realize at all. We can explain Peter's strange entry into Caiaphas's palace only from God's point of view, because God himself had positioned his church there in front of the door of the hall where her king received his sentence.

There, in that place, the same fiery apostle denied his master three times. Each time he did it in different words, the last time in even sharper and more embittered terms than the first two times. Of the different words he spoke, there is none that more terribly reveals what lived in his heart than the one phrase Mark has preserved for us: "I don't know the man you are talking about" (Mark 14:71).

"I don't know the man." We must remember the great significance of the term "knowing" in the Bible: it is always far more than simply an intellectual understanding; it always includes something of a more intense social relationship. "You only have I known of all the families of the earth; therefore I will punish you for all your sins" (Amos 3:2). "The Lord knows who are his" (2 Tim. 2:19). This is indeed that divine knowing on which we rely. And its counterpart is found in the urgent exhortation "In all your ways acknowledge him, and he will make your paths straight" (Prov. 3:6), and also in the wonderful prophecy "They will all know me, from the least of them to the greatest, declares the Lord" (Jer. 31:34). Associating with God involves a lifetime of uninterrupted knowing him and being known by him. The Savior himself said this in his instructions to the shepherd and the sheep: "I know my sheep and my sheep know me" (John 10:14). "The sheep follow [the good shepherd] because they know his voice" (John 10:4). It is always about "knowing" in that rich sense of having an unbreakable bond of deep and genuine communion. Peter himself expressed this sentiment when he said, "Lord, to whom shall we go? You have the words of eternal life. We believe and know that you are the Holy One of God" (John 6:68-69).

And then there are these devastating words: "I don't know the man." This can be understood in the most prosaic sense, of being unacquainted with or never having met the person; or in the sense that there is no meaningful relationship between that person and me; or "I don't know of a single instance when we ever met"; or "his life and mine have nothing in common, and we have lived totally apart from each other without ever encountering even mutual friends or interests; there simply is nothing that links us together."

"I Don't Know the Man"

How can Peter say this? His entire life of the last few years has been nothing else but getting to know Jesus and constantly learning of the greatness of his works. That has occupied his most profound thoughts; it has been the core of all his searching and hoping. His entire life has had only one goal: to know Jesus and to be known by him. Right from the moment Jesus saw him approaching and called him by his new name, that momentous name Peter, right from that very moment, Simon Peter, in the inmost recesses of his heart, was perfectly aware that he was known by Jesus. From that moment he had no greater desire than to get to know Jesus, in turn, in the unfathomable majesty of his divine being. His life had found its destiny in the mysterious reciprocity of knowing and being known. And that interaction had filled each of his days with wonderful surprises, and every day had revealed to him more and more glorious events. When he was on the mountain with Jesus and in childish ignorance had wanted to build three tents, one each for the master and his two celestial companions, at that moment he had learned to see Jesus in a completely new light. It was then that he was overcome by the glorious realization that at last he was beginning to *really* know — that he now *knew* in the true sense of the word.

So why would he now say that he does not know Jesus? We are not particularly concerned about discovering whether psychology can explain how a person can dig his own grave, can destroy the meaning of his existence, can undermine the very basis of his life and mind. That may be an interesting exercise, but in this night of all nights — now that all eras of world history converge into one focal point — other major happenings are at work. What does God have in mind? What is God's purpose here, now that he places the church right on the threshold of the hall where the king is about to be sentenced, where God has left the church in the lurch, a prey to the terrifying despair of her own unbelief? Why is this episode concerning the church placed in the center of Christ's suffering?

Peter is not an accidental individual here; he is much more than that. Here he pronounces what is in the deepest sense always present in the church — and thus also in us. We are here during that night of utter consternation ourselves, here in that palace of Caiaphas. The words spoken here are not some loose-lipped utterances. Here the most profound realities are revealed; here everything is shorn of all semblance of glamour:

here the ultimate truth has emerged: "I don't know the man." When we give this careful thought, it strikes us that in that dramatic night, when only the ultimate realities could exist, this was the hour when our *knowing* ceased to exist. It was then that our faith, our communion with Christ, our search for him, our service, our faith experience, our joy in God — all that disappeared in one instant, melted away as being unreal, unimportant, inadequate, and groundless. The only thing that held fast, the one item that remained valid in that night was the awesome knowledge that Jesus *knows* us. He entered into a living communion with us! That strong and sure knowing of Jesus — it stood there in that night as the only safe point, as the rock-solid ground on which everything rests.

The church of all ages, both in the past and yet to come, must be totally aware that it is not its knowing, its theology, its confessions that deserve the epitaph of "knowing," but only the "knowing" that Jesus understands will stand the test of time. In the night in which he was betrayed, there was, from the side of the church, only denial, rejection, cowardice, treason, escape, and rupture of every bond. But Jesus displayed his immense, totally encompassing "knowing," the kind that never fails, that is never shaken. In that grand night when all ages converged into one focal point, we did not contribute anything. The only thing that endured was his knowing with which he had known us in the mystery of his eternal love. All our own knowing of Jesus is nothing other than the fruit of his knowing. He held us fast, and by his holding us fast, we started to seek. We love him because he first loved us. In Caiaphas's palace our faith falls away: all that we had disappears, and only he stands firm.

All this should make an even greater impression on us when we recall what Adam said when he was summoned before God's tribunal. At that moment Adam was well aware of the relationship in which he found himself: a bond of solidarity with all humanity. But he used that solidarity to plead not guilty: "The woman you have given me." To be human is to stand in unison with all people; it is point and counterpoint; it is the interaction between knowing and being known. But in the perilous moments when life itself is at stake, Adam succumbs to the urge of self-preservation. He expresses solidarity then only as a means to find excuses: "My sin is only a moment in the immense collective sin, indicating that others have more guilt than I do." That is what Adam says, and so does the *adam* in all of us. It is so typically human. And Peter, having sneaked into Caiaphas's palace, as soon as he feels threatened, sings the same tune: "I don't know the man." In other words, "His sin is not my sin. I don't have to die his death. I don't have to share in his suffering. I really don't belong to him."

Peter retreats into the shelter of solitude, into the safety of detachment. That is the human in every human being. To sin is to seek self-preservation, to break from all solidarity with Christ. Only Jesus remains standing in total oneness with us all. He does not flee into loneliness, but keeps on embracing us all. His sin is our sin. His death is our death. His lostness is our lostness. That is the awesome legacy of Adam's sin: our sin is the refusal to know him as soon as our self-preservation is at stake. But Christ's grace is that he has known us exactly in our sin; he has suffered our suffering, has carried our doom, and died our death. In this night of all nights, only the most profound matters are expressed. Here *adam* disappears, and here the Christ of God stands in all his grandeur and beauty.

Failure to Confess

Peter's answer contains yet another aspect: the emphasis on Jesus' humanity. "I don't know the *man*." It is clear that using the word "man" here is not meant to imply anything inferior. It does not mean to belittle or insult. And yet this sharply uttered word of Peter contains, precisely in this context, something deeply sad. A few meters away, in Caiaphas's hall, at that very moment, the question is being debated whether he is more than just a man, whether he unjustly claimed to be the Son of God. That is the cardinal question in the palace of Caiaphas. The question is whether Jesus is human in the ordinary sense in which we all are human, whether his life is lived on the same level as ours, whether it exhausts itself in banalities and endless contortions to maintain the ineradicable human need for self-maintenance.

Is that also the theme of his life here on earth, or does his life in the world contain a new and mysterious element? Is it a prism through which Light Eternal breaks through onto this world and reveals itself to us in a rainbow of magnificent colors? Is it the visible manifestation of the invisible, the approachable embodiment of the unapproachable? Has eternity become time in him? Has the infinite put on the cloak of minuteness and even nothingness? Has he who rules from eternity to eternity come down into history as the Great Unknown? All this is at issue in this most terrible night of world history. Would it not have been marvelous if somewhere in the house of the high priest — perhaps somewhere in the inner court or in the humble quarters of the servants — if somebody had stood up and confessed: "This is the Christ, the Son of the living God."

Those words had once been spoken among the mountains of northern Palestine, where the snow-capped summits glistened in the bright light. That was a wonderful moment, but it would have had an infinitely greater impact if the church had stood here, in front of the door to the hall where this judicial process was taking place. The church should have spoken here and confessed: He is different, he is the *ganz Andere* (the "wholly other one"), different from all of us other mortals. It is utterly sad that the church had nothing else to say here than that utterly feeble "I don't know the man." To say that is to say that he is on the same level as all of us; he is just like us. Inside that hall the Son of man speaks his majestic witness: "From now on you will see the Son of man sitting at the right hand of the Mighty One and coming on the clouds of heaven." Here, at the entrance to the hall, the church on earth has nothing else to confess than this single phrase: "I don't know the *man*."

Why is this? Why does the church retract all her confessional statements? Why does she hide behind ignorance? And what does God have in mind with this happening on the night of all nights, when everything is reverting back to its deepest reality?

Could it be that our human confessions had to disappear in order that his magnificent and imperishable confession would prevail? When we failed to confess him before people, he confessed us before his Father in heaven. When we failed to acknowledge him, he knew us. When we placed him on our level and put him in our world, he came and stood in our place as a sinner and took upon himself our damnation. He stands there so that the church from here to eternity should realize that her knowledge and her confessions mean nothing at all, but that only his knowing, his confession, is the basis on which we rest. Our confession cannot be anything other than a reflection of his confessing, and our knowing can only be a mirror image of his knowing. Nothing of us remains upright in this calamitous night in Caiaphas's palace: everything has to be flattened to its very foundations. Nothing remains of our fancy words, and nothing is left for us to point to. Our input amounts to nothing other than unbelief and ignorance. But, towering above the ruins of our misery, there rises a faithfulness that is beyond our capacity to describe, displayed by him who embraces us when we push him away.

That is the message for us in Peter's denial. It is one of the most sorrowful events in the New Testament. Not our faith, not our most noble inclinations, not even our knowing of Jesus, amounts to anything as a basis for our salvation. We are not saved because of our faith, because of our confession, because we know Jesus. All these things are nothing by themselves; they are all worthless when weighed before God's face. Only Jesus saves us; only he knows us; only he confesses us. Our faith is only a response, only the fruit of his merciful knowing when we were still sinners. In the house of Caiaphas we are stripped of all our dignity, and our "flesh and blood" are displayed in their deepest stirrings. Only Christ remains. He knew us in that night of all nights. He saw us.

Our only hope and expectation is: "Now I know in part, then I shall know fully, even as I am fully known" (1 Cor. 13:12).

CHAPTER 8

The Sentence of the Governor

Judged Once, and Then Again

It is a strange and remarkable fact that Jesus was sentenced twice: first by the Sanhedrin, with Caiaphas presiding, and after that by Pontius Pilate, in the name of the emperor. But if we take the justice system of that time into account, it is not all that difficult to explain. During the Roman occupation (at the time Jesus was taken prisoner), the Sanhedrin had the authority to try cases; but in order to have the sentence verified, it needed the approval of a judge outside the Judaic judicial system — in this case, the Roman governor. So it is easy to explain why the Sanhedrin could not finalize the case with the rabbi of Nazareth without also involving the governor. Of course, the governor could have taken the easy way out and simply confirmed the Sanhedrin's sentence. For some reason (which the Gospel narratives do not explain), however, Pilate, the Roman governor at the time, preferred to deal with the matter independently and started to investigate whether the death sentence was indeed justified. That is the simple reason that we hear about two judicial processes in rapid succession, one at the priestly court and the other at the court of the governor.

From a historical perspective, therefore, this matter is not unusual at all. At most we may wonder why the governor went to so much trouble to make sure that justice would be done; but since we have no inkling what his motivation was, we will never know the answer. But it is an entirely different matter when we look at this question in the light of God's providential plan. Why did God split the process against Jesus in two, and why did God arrange this entire matter so that Jesus was sentenced not once, but twice? Why did God plan for the Savior of the world to be sentenced twice — on different grounds? The single sentence against Adam, against humanity at large, against the *adam* who had abandoned God in paradise, is split into two in the life of Jesus and divided over two different sentences. The only possibility is that God, in this double sentence, wants to tell us something that is of great significance.

As soon as our minds are open to considering these matters, we recall that the nature of sin shows two aspects, a priestly and a royal one. Adam's sin — our sin — is of a dual nature: on the one hand, it is a severing of the communion with God and claiming adherence to a new "god," which is the priestly part of the sin; on the other hand, this sin reveals itself also as breaking the connection with the harmonious and meaningful context of God's *kingdom* in his creation.

Mankind, alas, is totally out of tune with the symphony of the universe. We stubbornly have placed ourselves squarely over against the will of the one who reigns over all, the one whom all creatures obey. We are the rebels who dare to disobey God's royal will. We are the rebels who proclaim to be kings in our own right. Sin is the sundering of communion, and sin is rebellion and insurrection. Sin is fleeing from God's nearness; at the same time, sin is disobedience, refusing and resisting God's commands. These two facets of sin were quite easily detected in the humans' first sin, and they continue to dominate humanity's entire existence to this very day. When Adam and Eve wanted to be "like God, knowing good and evil," it meant a breach of communion with God and an escape from the light of his presence. And when that same couple, Adam and Eve, wanted to place their own human will over against the will of the Creator, that was desecrating the kingdom.

Throughout the ages, the two aspects of human life — the priestly and the royal — have preserved their distinctive features. We can clearly detect in Israel's history how God carefully arranged it so that these two would never mingle. True, Israel was both nation and church, that is, church in the form of a nation, so that these two — the priestly and the royal features — coincide. Nevertheless, God always kept these two clearly separated and has not wanted them to ever overlap. On the same Mount Zion were situated both the palace of the king and the Temple, where the high priest performs his official duty. However close they approached each other, they always remained distinct. When King Uzziah, in a fit of reckless pride and stupid daring, attempted to push the high priest aside and burn incense on the altar in the Lord's temple, he was not only severely reprimanded by the high priest but was also struck with leprosy, from which he suffered for the rest of his life and which forced him to live in isolation (2 Chron. 26:16-21). In some pagan nations the king is sometimes also the highest priest, the head of the cult. But in Israel, church and nation — however intimately they were connected — were nevertheless always sharply distinguished.

All this is, no doubt, also true of the dual sentence of Jesus Christ. The church had to sentence him by means of the high priest, and the nation had to do so through the office of the Roman governor. The church had to speak regarding the priestly aspect of the sin and the sundering of communion with God: Jesus had supposedly blasphemed God when he had called himself God's Son. And then the nation had to pronounce judgment on the royal aspect of sin: Jesus Christ had made himself king. The one sentence of humanity in Eden is split into two legal verdicts; in the one verdict, both sentences were included, because the rupturing of communion and the severing of the kingdom were seen as a single horrible transgression. However, in Jesus' life the two appear separately. That is why it pleased God to have Jesus judged twice.

The Legal Proceedings before the Governor

The legal wrangling before the court of the governor lasted for hours. Many difficulties arose, and time after time the proceedings took on new twists. In reconstructing how the different Gospels report the event, we can summarize it as follows. Early in the morning, the members of the Sanhedrin arrived at the court of the governor and accused Jesus of three serious crimes: (1) he taught the people heresies; (2) he told the people not to pay taxes to the emperor; (3) he claimed to be Christ, the king (Luke 23:2). All three accusations were of a political nature: they did not directly relate to religious wrongdoing, but they were couched in the kind of terms that Pilate could not dismiss.

Right from the start, however, it became clear that Pilate was not inclined to confirm the sentence of the Sanhedrin without further investigation. He decided to look into the matter more deeply. The first inquiry took place inside the gubernatorial palace. The main question there was whether Jesus had, indeed, claimed to be a king. At that session the Savior spoke the remarkable words to the effect that his kingdom was "not of this world" and that he had come "to testify to the truth" (John 18:36-37). Pilate got the impression from this that Jesus was an idealist, a utopian dreamer, and thus someone whom he could under no circumstances sentence as a politically dangerous criminal. He had Jesus brought outside, and he told the Jews who had congregated that he had found Jesus innocent. The Jews then shouted that Jesus had misled everybody — from Galilee to Judea. This outcry gave Pilate the excuse to send Jesus to Herod, because Herod was the tetrarch of Galilee. Since Jesus came from Galilee, he was under Herod's jurisdiction. That concluded the first part of the judicial proceedings.

The proceedings resumed when Jesus was taken from Herod's palace back to Pilate. At that point Pilate firmly resolved not to give in to the demand of the chief priests. He made up his mind and delivered his verdict: "Nothing this man has done calls for the death penalty. So I shall have him flogged, and then I shall release him" (Luke 23:16). That was the first sentence.

This announcement, however, caused the multitude gathered in front of the palace to embark on a loud and persistent show of disapproval. Pilate, attempting to mollify the public anger to some degree, and seeking a way out of his predicament, pitted Jesus against Barabbas, a murderer. In his heart, Pilate was completely convinced that the crowd out there would have enough feeling for justice to choose the release of Jesus over that of an out-and-out criminal who had been involved in an insurrection. However, Pilate's plan backfired: the crowd chose Barabbas over Jesus, and Pilate again faced the problem of what to do with Jesus. True to his first sentence, he commanded that Jesus be flogged. The soldiers who were ordered to do the flogging were given a free hand in carrying out this command: they took the liberty of portraying Jesus as a triumphant king, draping a purple mantle around him, putting a staff in his hands, and crowning him with thorns on his head. In this way he resembled a triumphant Christ, to whom all nations would someday be subject, the

Christus Triomphator (the triumphant king of Israel). When this despicable parody was over, Pilate thrust Jesus forward to show him to the unruly mob. With an undertone of pity in his voice, Pilate said, *Ecce homo* ("look at this man" [John 19:5]). If the governor had hoped that some of his own empathy would be imparted to the people out there, he was sadly mistaken. The mob was in an ugly mood, and their cry roared through the courtyard: "On the cross with him, crucify the villain!" The attempts of the weak governor were no match for the outpouring of furious rage by the rabble. It was now beyond him to further carry out the sentence he had once pronounced (partly fulfilled by the flogging) and to release Jesus. He again engaged in dialogue with the gathering in front of him, and with the chief priests, who were the inciting the crowd. That resulted in a new accusation: "We have a law, and according to that law he must die, because he claimed to be the Son of God" (John 19:7).

The political accusations abandoned, everything now focused on the religious charge that Jesus had made himself equal to God, thus blaspheming God. Before the judgment seat of Pilate, the same accusation that was brought before the Sanhedrin could now be heard — the allegation that started the second judicial process. Pilate was forced to interrogate Jesus once again, now on the issue of blasphemy. Again he brought Jesus inside and again asked him all kinds of questions. But this inquiry, too, led to nothing. Pilate could only conclude that this rabbi from Nazareth, who evidently managed to generate such intense anger amongst the priesthood, could under no circumstances be considered a politically dangerous agitator and revolutionary who deserved the imperial penalty. Once again Pilate took Jesus outside, and once again his voice echoed across the court of the palace: "I find him not guilty."

That does it! The chief priests were overcome by rage. They feared that their prey might yet escape them, and so now they used the ultimate threat as a way to get him into their clutches. "If you let this man go, you are no friend of Caesar. Anyone who claims to be a king opposes Caesar" (John 19:12). These last words contained a clear threat: If you dare to release this Jesus, we won't hesitate to lodge a complaint with the emperor and accuse you of allowing people who proclaim themselves king to run free. Thus, at long last, the accusation had taken on its final form. Here, before Pilate's tribunal, it all came down to the one cardinal indictment that Jesus had proclaimed himself king. All other accusations were pushed aside, and the whole trial concentrated on the one accusation: he is a rebel who proclaims himself to be king and thus he breaks the unity of the Roman Empire. And it is on the basis of that accusation that Jesus was sentenced. Not that he called himself Son of God; not that he had led the people onto the wrong path; not that he had told the people not to pay taxes — but simply that he had proclaimed himself king.

This is, in short, the gist of what happened during the court proceedings before Pilate's tribunal. The trial saw a number of dramatic moments, moments full of intense outbursts and massive tension. There were words loaded with infinite wisdom. The charge was often changed, rearranged, and differently formulated. But the result was that Jesus was convicted because he had declared himself king.

A few elements dominate this entire drama. First, there was Pilate's sense of justice: he knew the meaning of justice, and he stubbornly wanted to adhere to the code he knew. But he had no spine whatsoever. He started a dialogue with the mass of people when he should have adhered to the law he knew; when stern authority was necessary, he began to waver. He was totally unfit as a ruler — or a judge. We do not see in him a trace of true royalty: instead of taking the lead, he was led; instead of taking the initiative, he followed; instead of being a ruler of a nation, he was ruled by them. In spite of his official toga and the authority that went with his office, he was like a child at the mercy of the wiles of the mass. The ultimate cause of this weakness was his strong desire for self-preservation. He was afraid that, were he to carry out justice, it would cost him his position — perhaps his life. Above all, he wanted to maintain the status quo, and because of that desire, he forfeited his independence and became a slave of the masses.

The church pronounces her verdict on this weakling when she confesses, "Who suffered *under* Pontius Pilate." The creed does not say, "Who suffered *through* Pontius Pilate." Pilate was not even a direct actor in this terrible drama because he was nothing but a teetering wall, a gate that was easily crashed, under which he was crushed by the murderous multitude.

In contrast to Pilate's weakness was the strength of the chief priests' wrath. Not a trace of hesitation there, nor any fear. They tried all angles and kept on concocting new accusations as they withdrew the old ones.

They connived, they begged, they demanded, they yelled, they threatened — but in all this they only had their eyes on the one goal that they pursued with all their might. And because they single-mindedly went after this one objective, they gained the upper hand. The sentence was pronounced, and the "King of the Jews" was convicted. That is how, from a purely human perspective, matters took their course in this judicial standoff. Out of all this twisting and turning there finally emerged the charge that Jesus had proclaimed himself king, which earned him the death penalty. "He opposes the emperor," those of the Sanhedrin said. That is, he was breaking the unity of the empire.

Proclaiming Oneself King

It is not enough to rely only on these human factors, because they do not plumb the depth of these matters. God himself maintained the initiative in the proceedings, and from the very first God steered it so that one overriding accusation would emerge from all the charges. The compass needle of the accusation swayed back and forth until it finally settled on the one unforgivable crime: he proclaimed himself king. That's the way God had always wanted it.

Why did God desire that Jesus should be sentenced on the basis of this particular accusation? Because this was Adam's sin (*adam*, the human in every human being) and thus it was our sin, our sin from birth. God did not want Jesus to be sentenced because he had told others not to pay taxes to the emperor. That was a side issue — too historically conditioned, not nearly central enough. God did not want Jesus to be sentenced because he had led others astray, since that would fail to pinpoint the core of human sin. Finally, God did not want Pilate to sentence Jesus because he had called himself God's Son. That priestly accusation had been dealt with before the tribunal of the Sanhedrin and had resulted in a sentence by the high priest. Here, with Pilate as the empire's judge, only one accusation remained valid: he had proclaimed himself king. That was Adam's sin, and it was on this ground that Jesus was sentenced. John 19 has to take back what was written in Genesis 3, and Genesis 3 has to be covered over by John 19.

The Sentence of the Governor

Proclaiming oneself king in the context of the Roman Empire meant to incite revolution. It meant to rip apart the bundle of powers that symbolized Rome's imperial structure. When a private person, without divine permission, dares to assume royal prerogatives, it signifies rebellion against the legal authority that has God's mandate to govern. It really means rebellion against God himself. When a person makes himself king, he declares his autonomy and renounces obedience to the true king.

However, in the broader context of God's eternal kingdom, the act of proclaiming oneself to have royal status has an entirely different aspect. It ruptures the harmonious, cosmic coherence of the kingdom by unilaterally declaring independence and placing oneself at the center. This indicates an escape from the meaningful context of God's all-encompassing marvelous creation. Those who declare themselves king pretend to be capable of judging between good and evil. For example, they assume that they can eat from the Tree of the Knowledge of Good and Evil, and they declare themselves to be independent from God. They choose their own ways, they separate themselves from the centripetal powers that hold the universe together, and they seek their own point of departure — one that starts in their own selves.

In the great scheme of creation, God had given humanity a degree of royal dignity, but that royal office was subordinate to his authority and subject to acting in harmony with the only-wise will of God, in order not to disturb matters and bring about chaos or disorientation. But this unilateral royal self-proclamation that humanity assumed has indeed disturbed the creation order, has led to universal dissolution — from decay to total collapse. From now on, humans do what is good in their own eyes, determining what is acceptable and what is not. And each further step entails further fights against the mighty will of him who maintains the course of suns and stars and rules as the only sovereign over the oceans and the continents. Jesus is sentenced because he proclaimed himself king, the underlying cause of all human sin. Jesus is sentenced and condemned because he is Adam, the human in all humans: he represents all of us.

All this is quite simple to understand in the light of the *Urzeit* and what happened at the commencement of all human history. When we consider what the real meaning of the history of the world is, then our perspective becomes totally different and much more beautiful. As we have seen, the history of the world is determined by the never-ending attempt on the part of the human race to erect a human empire and so to attain harmony through a united effort, and all that on the basis of human sovereignty — thus totally apart from God. In other words, it is another effort to build the Tower of Babel. The real miracle is that, straight through all these strivings to arrive at a human-dominated empire, God reestablishes his eternal, unequaled kingdom. That is the ultimate meaning of history.

The prophets of old Israel were steadfast in expressing their confidence that God would realize his kingdom through Israel and through the Messiah, the true David who would sprout from Israel. This Messiah, as the real ruler of Israel, would not only govern his own people with justice, but would also make all nations subject to him. That would partly take place by physical force; but, in spite of that, this domination would prove to be an imperishable blessing for these other peoples. "In those days ten men from all languages and nations will take hold of one Jew by the hem of his rope and say, 'Let us go with you, because we have heard that God is with you'" (Zech. 8:23). The Gentiles will come entirely of their own free will, they will joyfully bow down before Israel's king, and thus will Yahweh's kingdom in this world be restored. Once this kingdom is restored in the world, the entire creation will share in this, as is witnessed in the following words: "The wolf will live with the lamb, and the leopard will lie down with the goat. . . . They will neither harm nor destroy on all my holy mountain, for the earth will be full of the knowledge of the Lord as the waters cover the sea" (Isa. 11:6, 9). These were the expectations of the prophets of old.

So here we have the long-expected king of Israel, the real David, the Messiah. He did not unilaterally claim his royal office, but God called him to rule over Israel. During the years of his sojourn he proclaimed the establishment of the kingdom of God. Never did he seek anything for himself, because he always had one goal: that Israel's God would have total dominion. It was always God's intention that world history would find its realization in the Son. He did what the prophets of old had foretold. But instead of Israel's recognizing and honoring him, and together with him proclaiming divine kingship over the world, it placed itself over against him as one man and denounced him for having not only proclaimed himself king but also for having offended the Roman emperor.

The Sentence of the Governor

With those last denouncing words, Israel forfeited its own hope forever, because that same emperor was, after all, none other than the pagan ruler who unlawfully exercised dominion over the Lord's inheritance. The emperor was not the bearer of God's kingship but the self-deifying power who did not acknowledge Yahweh's higher power. Israel counted speaking against the emperor as Jesus' sin, and to resist the emperor was, in the eyes of Israel, a crime worthy of the death penalty. Israel no longer knew what it should be expecting; Israel no longer understood what God's purpose was for his people; Israel no longer saw the kingship of Yahweh as the greatest of all prophecies.

All this is the final straw for Israel being a nation in its own right. The only purpose for Israel's existence was that, out of it, Yahweh would establish his dominion over the earth. Moses had strived for that, and Joshua, Gideon, David, and Hezekiah had all wrestled with the overwhelming pagan powers that threatened to wipe out Israel. Its own existence was never the issue, because Israel's status as a nation was only a means to accomplish that far greater goal: Yahweh's kingship over the entire world. Israel never succumbed to nationalism in the usual sense of the word because it had always understood that it was the medium to a much higher goal of Yahweh's kingship coming into the world. But now that Israel's king has appeared at last, in whom and through whom God intended to bring his dominion into the world, now Israel exclaims, "We do not want him; he has proclaimed himself king and has spoken out against the emperor." At that same moment the very existence of Israel has become an empty formula, and Israel loses the very basis of its existence. If Israel no longer is the instrument through which God brings about his kingdom in the world, then it is reduced to nothing. Then it has lost its purpose and is limited to foolishness and vanity. There, before Pilate's judgment seat, Israel, as a nation, commits suicide by killing off the ultimate basis for its existence.

Yet, through all this, the predictions of the old prophets have come true. Through Jesus, David's son, through the Jesus who has sprung from the old nation of Israel, God will build his kingdom in the world. Many nations will be united under the scepter of the Messiah. Paul and Silas, Peter and John, they all experienced that "ten men from diverse tongues and nations grabbed the hem of their coat, saying, let us go with you because we have heard that God is with you." The prophecy was indeed fulfilled, but it was totally different from what had been Israel's expectation: it would come to pass, not through Israel as a nation, but through its destruction, through its downfall.

Still, we have not yet gauged the full extent of this great and mysterious moment. If we want to understand what really took place here, we must look at the entire picture. We are dealing here with God's kingdom which, in Jesus Christ, claims the entire world. Through Jesus, God proclaims his kingdom over the world and causes his creation to be subject to him. This is the very moment when God proclaims his own eternal kingdom, while stoutly opposing the human version. Israel's answer is the human answer: the promotion of human dominion. Israel's reply is the reply of humanity itself because Israel *is* Adam, the human in every human being. The judicial process before Pilate signifies the crisis of the Lord's kingship in the world. This is where they face each other, where it is human rule versus the Lord's. Jesus' sentence pronounced here amounts to a sentence of God himself because he has proclaimed himself king. We can only tolerate a kingdom that is founded on the basis of our own apostasy from God, our autonomy. We feel at home under such circumstances, because through it we can express what people usually think. That way we can give direction to what everybody else secretly desires — totally in tune with our hidden longings.

Such a king embodies precisely what everybody wants: he is Adam, king by the grace of the human will. We like to offer our obeisance to such a king. In the name of our own kingship the people of Israel pronounce sentence over God's demand for obedience: "He has proclaimed himself king." Christ does not rule the way we do. He stands far above our deepest expression of human life and thinking. We, the human race, trying the best we can, shout out, "We do not want him to be king over us." "The kings of the earth take their stand, and the rulers gather together against the Lord and against his anointed one. 'Let us break their chains,' they say, 'and throw off their fetters'" (Ps. 2:2-3). The Gospel of John expresses the infinitely tragic in these moving words: "He was in the world, and though the world was made through him, the world did not recognize him. He came to that which was his own, but his own did not receive him" (John 1:10-11). King Adam, who had placed himself illegally on the throne and thus had broken the harmonious interconnectedness of the universe, says to God: "He has made himself king and opposes the emperor; he is against us, against what we long for and want at all cost. He is not a king by the grace of us, but he, by himself, has taken the kingship upon him."

What takes place before Pilate's palace is the nadir of human sin, sin in its most ferocious form. What was merely a whisper in Eden is expressed here as a thousand times magnified, cascading across Jerusalem as it echoes through numberless mouths. Here the kingdom of Yahweh collides with the kingdom built by human hands. And Yahweh's kingdom is rejected: it is decried as revolution, as sin incarnate, as usurpation and rebellion. Seen from the perspective of the sinful mind, God himself is the greatest sinner and the real rebel. He is guilty and must die. Here we are faced with a crisis of world-historical proportions; here all authorities converge, and the fate of the universe hangs on a thread. Here the King Eternal stands before the judgment seat of mortal men, the creatures he has made, and they castigate him for proclaiming himself king, king by the grace of his sovereign will, by the grace of . . . himself.

It is all totally perplexing. The gates of hell are open. It seems as though the entire world will collapse, as though everything will be reduced to nothing. The entire creation is confused, and everything is upside down. The shackled God is accused of revolution, and unshackled humanity shouts victory. Here the nonsense to crown all nonsenses is displayed, the folly of all follies. It is so unfathomably crazy and confused that we can cry our hearts out, deeply saddened by the insanity of our existence, by the tragedy of all tragedies.

The King Is Sentenced

However, we must go on. The mystery of "the reverse side of the coin" has been such a prominent feature of this passion drama that it calls upon us to try to understand what God really has in mind. For looks are deceiving. The demonic cooperation between the powerless Pilate and the vulgar villains, the chief priests, is in fact nothing other than the final sentencing on behalf of God. During this entire episode, God is the judge. It is not Pilate, because he doesn't have any clue as to what is really going on. He is a mere bystander who, when push comes to shove, crawls away into the safe haven of self-preservation. Nor is it the chief priests, because, for all their knowledge of Scripture, they have not seen anything of the glory of the anointed of God. The only judge in this entire dispute is God, with the accused being none other than Adam, humanity — all of us.

When the verdict is delivered, based on the accusation that he has proclaimed himself king, it is God who pronounces this against Adam, against us. Here again is paradise, the continuation of what had started in Eden. In Christ our sin is called by its name. That sin is that we have blasphemed God and have made ourselves equal to him. That was the priestly part of our sin: breaking communion. That he proclaimed himself king is the royal part of our sin, the breach in the harmonious unity of God's magnificent world. Those were our sins — we did all that.

No person in this court case is what he or she appears to be. Pilate and the chief priests together are Adam: both have deified themselves and now personify the self-proclaimed kings. Yet they represent God, for they are "gods" in the Old Testament sense of the word. They stand here in the place of God. In this judicial dispute they are God: that is, they are what they are not. Here Christ is God, God's claim to kingship over the world; but in this dispute he is humanity, *adam*, the human in all human beings. He stands there in the place of all humanity, and he is what he is not. This contest is true in a double sense: it is both the greatest possible sin, where sin meets its match and where all possible variations of sin meld together, and also the most impressive display of God's grace. Here Christ replaces Adam, striding past the flaming sword, letting himself be scorched and destroyed so that we may gain access to that miracle of atonement, where the cherubim are — now without their swords — reverently bowing before God's holy and redemptive will.

It is possible to draw all kinds of conclusions from the saga of Christ's suffering. We can conclude that it was one insane eruption of hellish powers. Or we can detect in it the cacophony of demonic blasphemy. But we also can see it as the moment when the full extent of God's powers, evident in his everlasting love for sinners, converges into a single focus, the suffering of the Son of man. Here we see the infinite depth of grace and love; here we stand face to face before God. When every road was blocked, God opened up the way to eternal redemption in Christ.

Just when God's kingdom seemed to be overrun by the human kingdom, when God himself was convicted of rebellion, it was in that very moment that God confirmed his kingdom. Through his suffering and death God deploys his kingdom so that there, in that very kingdom, he will bring together all parts of the universe, so that, at the end of days, every knee shall bow before Jesus Christ the Lord, to the glory of God the Father.

CHAPTER 9

The Death of Humanity

Death

When we talk about the death of Christ, we sense that, as so often before, we must abandon our everyday, cliché-prone Western way of expression and instead embrace the language of Scripture. Influenced by scientific thinking that has infiltrated our entire life in the Western world, especially in the last two centuries, and has affected all strata of life, the implications of the term "death" have been immensely weakened. Death has become an ordinary and normal physical phenomenon, something that is part of life in this world and that can be explained by purely physical factors.

This simple scientific explanation of death was not unknown in antiquity. Many different philosophical movements in the Greek world explained death, just as I have above, as a normal happening that is rather unpleasant but nevertheless quite natural. Life and death inevitably are closely related, so much so that when we say "life" we say "death." Still, in antiquity the concept of death was associated with all kinds of mythical and often fantastic notions. Not until the persistent infiltration of the scientific point of view, so typical of our modern culture, was the concept of death robbed of all deeper meaning and made into a normal occurrence not really worth any further thought. It used to be that an animal died, but a man or woman "passed away." Passing away was seen as something different from, something more than, plain dying. Nowadays we are inclined to do away with that distinction and simply say that both humans and animals die, and that death, from a physical point of view, is completely explainable.

We have to let go of this shallow way of thinking when we are dealing with the death of Christ, which is in essence the death of humanity. In the Bible the word "death" still has the connotation of something terrible — not something normal and self-explanatory. Take, for example, the woman from Tekoa, who said to David: "Like water spilled on the ground which cannot be recovered, so we must die" (2 Sam. 14:14). By putting it that way, she characterized death as something inescapable and irrevocable; yet she certainly did not negate the mystery and fearful character of death. Death is not something natural; on the contrary, it is far more the denial of all that is natural, reversing the laws of natural life. Death is something beyond our understanding, something so abhorrent that it simply cannot be grasped.

The odiousness of death is expressed quite succinctly in the somber words of Psalm 88: "Like one alone among the dead; like the slain lying in their graves; like those you remember no more, cut off, as they are, from your hand" (Ps. 88:6, The Grail translation). Death means that we are severed from the hand of Yahweh, the king of life; it means that Yahweh no longer remembers us, that we are cut loose from the eternal sources of light and life. Death is darkness. These few words make it quite clear that the concepts of both death and life are treated in the Bible in theological terms: that is, they both refer back to God. The Old Testament saints saw life as walking in the light of God's face, praising God and serving him. Death is the denial of all that determines human life, because "the dead shall not praise the Lord, not those who go down into the silence" (Ps. 115:17). There the voice of praise is stilled, and the joyful service of the Lord comes to an end. In death is only silence and darkness.

In keeping with this concept, death is often portrayed in the Bible as a special realm, a territory where the dead carry on their dark existence. There, in the realm of the dead — also called Sheol — all laughter and jubilation cease; no room is found there for that joie de vivre that determines the essence of life, since the glow of God's face does not penetrate there. Those who enter there, those who go down through the portals of Sheol, turn their back on all earthly pleasure and all the good things the Lord in his grace wants to impart to his children on earth. They are torn from the Lord's hand, and the Lord does not remember them anymore. In that dark realm, King Death rules, the one who tightly controls his territory and does not tolerate the return of anyone in his grip to the land of the living. For the Israelite of the Old Testament, the single word "death" contained a world of anxiety and despair.

Behind that despair lay people's awareness that there existed an unbreakable connection between sin and death. Sin was seen as nothing short of severing communion with God and fleeing from his face. That was the root cause of death. That showed death in all its horror. Sin, after all, is to leave the meaningful context of God's kingdom. But once we have done this — once we have chosen to be outside God's kingdom — where do we find a place to stand, where do we cast our anchor? We do not possess the source of life. To voluntarily leave the kingdom means to be mired in outer darkness, where there is weeping and gnashing of teeth. In other words, sin and death are in essence the same because death is nothing other than the continuation of the process that had its start in sin. Paul says, without any reservation, that death is the end, the *telos* (that is, the natural outcome) of sin (Rom. 6:21). "Sin, when it is full-grown, gives birth to death" (James 1:15). It is not true that we sin and that then, from an outside source, death overwhelms us. No, by abandoning God, by purposely leaving his kingdom, we embrace the clutches of death. Outside God there is no life. When Adam, the human in every human, is expelled from paradise, banned from the Tree of Life and communion with God, who created us all, then the only option is death. All avenues we now pursue will only end up in death.

Death in its deepest essence is irrevocable. Nobody returns from Sheol. Once we are in the grip of the king of all terrors, we can never escape from his grip. In the ancient systems of Eastern philosophy, everything was relative: life and death overlapped each other; a person could die and later be reborn; the boundaries between life and death were mere pencil lines, vague dividers, easily erased everywhere. In the Bible everything is unconditional. Those who live — that is, those who are before the face of Yahweh, who serve him and are included in his kingdom — live in the ultimate sense of the word. But those who die — that is, those who fall away from God's face, who break away from his kingdom — become the prey of death for eternity. The Bible sees all these matters in that ultimate light that strikes us as strange and bewildering. In the Bible there is no return from Sheol, no way back to the light of God's presence. It is moving forever and ever on the sinister road from death to death, from darkness to darkness. In theology we have made distinctions between physical death, spiritual death, and eternal death. These three are, in the deepest meaning of the language of the Bible, identical. Death is the ultimate defeat: it means to sink forever into the realm of silence and darkness.

There is escape, but the Old Testament contains only a few vague hints of such deliverance. It is possible that God "will not leave my soul among the dead" (Ps. 16:10), that "God will ransom me from death and take my soul to himself" (Ps. 49:15); "You were holding me by my right hand, you will guide me by your counsel and so lead me to glory" (Ps. 73:23-24). But the release from the realm of death is a mystery of God's grace. The believers of the Old Testament saw it but did not understand it. The mystery was only fully realized in Jesus Christ.

The Road to Golgotha

We must resume the saga of Christ's suffering and follow him on his *via dolorosa* to his death on the cross. Again, it will be impossible to deal with all the details as relayed to us in the Gospels, so we shall limit ourselves to the main points. Though the Gospels tell us very little about the road to Golgotha, they all do emphasize that Jesus himself, at least initially, carried the cross on which he would be nailed. That brief moment, loaded with shame and deep humiliation, shows that he was forced to cooperate personally in carrying out his sentence. It was apparently the custom that criminals who were sentenced to die on the cross were forced to shoulder the very torture instrument on which they soon would suffer and die. In the case of Jesus, this custom was fraught with tragic symbolism. He was made an accomplice in his own execution, an assistant in carrying out his own sentence. He surrendered himself to death and subjected himself to what God wanted him to undergo. His voluntary acceptance of the punishment for sin could not be better illustrated than through this shameful and detestable humiliation.

Apart from his carrying of the cross, the Gospels also focus on the words Jesus spoke on the road to Golgotha. Luke mentions that Jesus addressed those Jerusalem women who were mourning him: "For the time will come when you will say, 'Blessed are the barren women, the wombs that never bore and the breasts that never nursed.' Then they will say to the mountains, 'Fall on us and to the hills, cover us'" (Luke 23:29-30). It is clear that Jesus here refers to the coming fall of Jerusalem, the precursor of the apocalypse. Now that the high priest has given the true sacrifice (Jesus) over to death, the Temple has become a meaningless edifice, a hollow ornament — without significance and without value. Now that Israel has condemned its great king to death, this also means that its royal residence has degenerated into an empty symbol. Jerusalem has lost its significance now that the coming king is sentenced within its walls, reducing Israel's story to folly, especially now that its ultimate historical purpose, that of the coming of its king, has been totally rejected by the screaming mob. Jerusalem and the Temple still exist, but they are emptied of their content. They stand there against the blue sky as meaningless letters, as words without content. Soon they both will be wiped away, as useless, by God. That is how Jesus, in the hours of his bitter suffering, saw the terrible consequences of his death for the city where singing pilgrims had so often praised their communion with Israel's God.

What follows, in a few short sentences, is the actual crucifixion, the particulars of which I cannot go into here except to point out the curse that is connected to death on the cross: "Anyone who is hung on a tree is under God's curse" (Deut. 21:23). That sentence in Deuteronomy could not, at the time, be applied to the death on the cross, because that form of execution was not practiced in those early days of Israel; rather, it refers to death by hanging. What applied to hanging was also valid for death on the cross, and Paul applies it without any hesitation (Gal. 3:13). It is difficult to now trace why death by hanging was so severely cursed. One probable reason was that death by hanging severs the connection with the earth that feeds us all. Numerous nations still maintain the ceremony of treating a small child with special rituals when it first gets into touch with the fertile earth. This contact with the earth is an essential element of life. We are taken from the earth, we belong to the earth, and we live through the earth. Our bond with the earth is so strong that we cannot for a moment imagine existing apart from the earth, and hanging breaks the contact with the earth. Hanging from a tree places a person outside the great cosmic unity and puts him all by himself as an exile, outside the wider context of God's glorious creation. That is why hanging is an eloquent expression of being expelled from God's kingdom. When suspended above the earth, human beings are placed outside the contact with the earth. Humans, as exiles and lonely lost souls, are carried outside the powerful context of God's life-energizing grace, which is the significance of that dreadful death on the cross. Scripture, rather than emphasizing that death on the cross is painful, points out that it foreshadows the cruel reality of carrying God's curse.

Words on the Cross

It will never be possible for us to sense the meaning of the various details that the Gospels describe for us about the crucifixion. When we talk about Christ's suffering on the cross, we always emphasize the grief and the pain Jesus must have felt. Scripture never does that. Scripture never draws our attention to the subjective side of things, the agony that Jesus went through on the cross. Instead, Scripture always points out the objective side, what actually happened — referring to the curse and the death. That even applies to Jesus' clothes. John is quite explicit about how the soldiers divided Jesus' vestments and cast lots for who would get Jesus' seamless garment, woven in one piece from top to bottom (John 19:23-24).

This tiny episode is difficult for us to understand because we have forgotten, in our Western way of thinking, what the purpose of a garment is. We wear clothes to cover this or that part of our body; clothes are in some mechanical fashion tied to the body, but they do not form a part of it. People in the East see clothes as being an integral part of the body. Clothing is a self-expression of the person and forms a unity with the human persona. When their hearts are torn with grief, Eastern people tear their clothes; when their hearts are anxious and bowed down with misery, they put on "sackcloth and ashes." When the witch of Endor saw the shadow of Samuel arise from the earth, she recognized him by his wearing the mantle of a prophet. The woman who had suffered so many years touched the edge of Jesus' garment (Luke 8:44) and was healed. The saints in the Temple wear long white garments (Rev. 7:9). Clothes are always much more than mere body covers because they reveal something of the human soul, something of their strength and their life. Therefore, the clothes are a mirror of the person. Somehow we can still sense a bit of that when one of our loved ones has died, and we are reluctant to use the clothes of that person for different purposes.

When we take all this into account, we can understand what it meant when the rough soldiers, under the very eyes of Jesus, divided his clothes and cast lots for his garment. Here Jesus is treated like a piece of merchandise, an item in an auction that can be gambled away as a thing of no account. Greater humiliation is hardly possible. That is why this facet of the suffering of the Messiah was already mentioned in the Old Testament as an abhorrent sign of the depth of his degradation (Ps. 22:18).

The cross had a sign at the top that said: "Jesus of Nazareth, King of the Jews." This nameplate was, in essence, nothing but Pilate's childish act of vengeance toward the stubborn chief priests. When he was forced to sentence Jesus because Jesus had proclaimed himself king, Pilate wanted to rub it in, emphasizing with that inscription that Jesus hung there as "King of the Jews." In so doing he hit the Jews not only in their national pride but also in the expectations that they still greatly treasured as a nation.

But that caption also had a deeper meaning. God, too, had wanted this to happen, for Jesus to be crucified because he was the king of the Jews. It was not that he *pretended* to be so; no, it was because he, in fact, was that. As the king of the Jews he had to undergo the suffering that already had been foretold in the Old Testament concerning the son of David. The heading "King of the Jews" also contained, according to the continuous line of thinking in Scripture, the title "King of the World." That was why the inscription was written in three languages (John 19:20). Jesus was indeed "king of the world." He was the king through whom God reestablished his eternal, imperishable kingdom in the world. He was the king in whom God reunited the world as a mighty entity under his scepter. The meaning of this inscription was not that Jesus was the king of the world and nevertheless was being crucified; rather, its meaning was that he entered death precisely *as* king of the world. His kingship over the world would be based on the redemption of the world and would be established in his suffering and death, able to come to full realization only via his suffering.

A few words on the cross refer back to this kingship in striking terms.

Luke tells us that one of the two criminals who were suspended on each side of Jesus chastised his fellow prisoner because of his blasphemy. Then this man, in simple and moving words, addressed Jesus: "Remember me when you come into your kingdom." This man saw something then and there that was still hidden from everybody else: they could not see that his cross was not the great fiasco of his kingship, but that it somehow was a phase through which his kingdom would come. Jesus' death sentence did not prevent God's plan for the world but was rather a moment in the divine plan of the kingdom. It belonged to it and was an inseparable part of it. No one in the crowd — and not even any of the disciples — fathomed this at the time. This particular murderer, who was on the brink of death, saw this more sharply and more deeply than all the others. Nor did it escape him that the crown of thorns resting on Jesus' head was equal to a real royal crown. He saw right through the bluster of the soldiers when they gambled away his garment, an act that in no way diminished the royal aura emanating from Jesus. With a clarity that can only astound us, this man begged Jesus to remember him when he entered *into his kingdom*. That kingdom is not some little affair next to other minor principalities, and it can under no circumstances be compared to Sheol, the realm of the dead. "Your kingdom" can be nothing other than the restored universe, the cosmos now in its full glory, rearranged under the one head, united again in a meaningful relationship under the rule of the Son of man. Those who are part of the reborn universe, in that universal kingdom — they live! Their lives have regained their purpose and reattained their goal. They know themselves to be a tiny part of the totality of things, a single note in the overwhelming new world symphony. This murderer on the cross had an inkling of this: he understood how, through Jesus' death, cosmic unity would become reality, and how Jesus would become king through the cross and through death.

Jesus' answer to the murderer is utterly remarkable. Not for one minute does Jesus dispute the truth about the kingdom. Yet he does not refer back to the word "kingdom" but replaces it with the word "paradise": "I tell you the truth, today you will be with me in paradise" (Luke 23:43). The word "paradise" evokes a world of memories and in one stroke brings us back to the *Urzeit* of humanity. We again hear the burbling of the water of life; we again see the Tree of Life, rising stately and high, loaded with

God's promises. Paradise is the unspoiled world where the total harmony of all creatures entwines everything into intimate cohesion. Paradise is the kingdom as seen by God on the morning of creation, when he saw all that he had made and behold, it was very good. Paradise! To be sure, it was barred by cherubim whose flaming swords guarded the Eastern gate; but in reality, paradise never went away. The Holy of Holies was a permanent reality in the midst of Israel, cordoned off by tightly woven curtains and guarded by the true watchmen of God's holiness.

That paradise is the world now open for Jesus and his kingdom. After all, he is Adam, the human being to whom God had deeded paradise. No, that paradise is not the realm of the dead, even though it is situated behind the dark gate of death. Neither is it the heaven where God dwells. It is the whole creation renewed, the cosmos in which heaven and earth are joined together in one accord and where everything is again ordered and subjected to the will of the one who rules over all. "Today you will be there!" That means that today all these long centuries disappear; today the numbering of the years ceases; today you are, in one movement, where the cradle of humanity stood. And there you will be, together with me. But now paradise is different, because it is a paradise with Jesus. Something is left, however, that is a reminder of those long centuries of history, the nightmare of wars and sickness and death, and that is Jesus the Redeemer. You will not be there all by yourself, but you will stand there with me, the Redeemer, and I will be your guide in that paradise, in a world of pure light.

That one sentence that Jesus spoke on the cross gives a wholly different meaning to the cross and everything taking place around it. Golgotha lies next to paradise; there is only an extremely thin curtain separating Calvary from paradise. That curtain has to be pierced, and then paradise opens up with unfathomable riches and glory. None of the mocking crowd notices it, and not even the disciples detect it. Only Jesus sees it — and that one murderer who is standing at the borderline between two worlds.

The Gospels, in addition to Jesus' royal pronouncement, also mention Jesus' outcry, revealing the utmost of his immense suffering as priest. "About the ninth hour Jesus cried out in a loud voice, *Eloi, Eloi, lama sabachtani,* which means, "My God, my God, why have you forsaken me?" (Matt. 27:46). Of all the words spoken on the cross, these are the most touching but also the most mysterious. Here death is being experienced in the utmost and bitterest sense of the word. This is death. This is the experience of being pulled out of the safety of the Father's hand and being wiped out of everybody's memory. For a moment everything becomes murky, as dense dark clouds gather over the misery-laden land of Judah, where, in the heart of this blackness, Jesus hangs on a cross. Gloom crawls inside his heart and filters to the depth of his soul, penetrating through every pore of his being. God's light, which a moment ago embraced the entire world like a mighty dome, is now far away — out of Jesus' sight. Jesus hangs there, abandoned in the total emptiness of a God-less world. Below him yawns the bottomless abyss of hell, the absoluteness of total abandonment and darkness, without a single ray of light. He hangs there, feeling as if nothing exists outside him, as if there is only emptiness, the infinite emptiness of a universe without meaning, without light, without sense.

Sin, from the very first, was nothing but a breaking of communion with God and a desire to go it alone. No sooner did humanity venture to be equal to God than it cut off the lifeline by which its existence was connected to God. There the human race would stand, as solitary figures, abandoned by God. Humanity had pushed God away, the very basis on which its tiny feet rested, and now the human race was suspended in a complete vacuum, in absolute abandonment. That was sin, and this still is sin. At one time Adam had embraced this aloneness as his greatest possession, without ever realizing that, outside God, there is no safe haven anywhere. The *adam* in all of us, the humanness in every human being throughout mankind's very long life so far, seeks aloneness as the only ground on which to stand.

To be just oneself — that is, to make oneself the focal point of one's own senses and thoughts — that is being a god to oneself, even if it is nothing but a caricature of God. That is abandonment, the level on which the human race lives and stirs and acts. The reason we do not experience this aloneness as a deep pain is that the rays of God's infinite mercy still play a role in our lives and still warm us through God's wonderful glow. But the time comes when the divine rays retreat and the divine light recedes, when all that is left is absolute aloneness. Then, from the recesses of our hearts, an inexpressible angst slowly rises, a terrible despair, a despondency that we sometimes experience in our nightmares, a hopelessness that chokes off our breathing and paralyzes us to the core of our being. It is a form of rejection that is the death that constantly lurks around us until its grip ultimately strangles us.

It is this abandonment, this indescribable dread and anxiety, that now envelops Jesus. In this he is Adam, humanity personified, the person who claimed to be God but broke all communion with God. And the consequence is that all the terror that eventually had to come, now inevitably descends on him.

This abandoning is far more terrible than what had just occurred in Caiaphas's residence and in Pilate's palace. There it was also God who sentenced Adam, but there it was somehow drowned out by a multitude of human voices. Here it is nobody but God. And that one God now turns his face away from the Son of man, withdraws his hand, and lets him fall into the measureless depth of lostness. From the totality of his being, he groans and moans to heaven: "My God, my God, why have you forsaken me?" There are no human intermediaries here, nothing left to divert attention or offer distraction. There is nothing here but the single, all-consuming abandonment as the God of life withdraws from the human race. In this complete isolation, nobody can breathe, nobody can live, nobody can find a place to stand. The Son of man feels himself sinking away, faster and faster, into infinite depths. Here the heart ceases to beat, the whole body shudders, and slowly but surely, with inexorable outcome, death will come to swallow its prey.

Immediately after this heart-rending cry of abandonment, light again breaks out all over. In the pitch-black darkness, rays of light burst forth. Golgotha's silhouette is again visible, in all its barrenness and horror, against the background of the ramparts and palaces of Jerusalem in the distance. The world emerges again from the night into which it had disappeared.

Not long after this, Jesus speaks his last words. First the tremendous shout of joyful victory: "It is accomplished!" After that the last words of surrender: "Father, into your hands I commend my spirit."

The Mystery of the Cross

When we stand at the foot of the cross, the full impact of the mystery of Jesus' death overwhelms us. Here all pieces of the world's puzzle come together; here we stand at the outermost edge of our knowing and understanding. In the first place, it is striking that what happens on Golgotha is the completion of the Fall into sin. God enters the world in Christ. He grabs the world in his powerful hands in order to return it to the unity that held it together at one time. In Christ, God places the full authority of his kingdom in the heart of the world. God's grip targets us, requires from us that we fully submit to his will, and wants us to bow down before his majesty.

Golgotha spells out our response in a few short episodes. We push God's hand away with all the force we can muster. Humanity takes God and discards him, casting him into the outermost darkness, plunging him into the infinite depth of death. Long ago, humanity placed itself outside the communion with God, wanting to live by itself and for itself. Humanity dared to design its own kingdom, where it wanted to garner all powers into a harmonic whole. And humanity continues to persist in this fatal act until the bitter end. When God enters this human kingdom and proclaims his own kingdom and power, he is forcibly removed from the worldly domain and hanged on a rough piece of wood and driven back to the realm of the dead. Imagine humanity being alive and God being dead! The human kingdom of make-believe, of misery, of fraud and hate, of death and destruction, is triumphant. Golgotha seals the collision between the two kingdoms.

There is another view. Here, on Golgotha, we are dealing with Christ, who is the great mediating high priest, the bridge between God and humanity. He represents humanity over against God, claiming solidarity with the human race and confronting God in the name of humanity. In him humanity again approaches the throne of God, while at the same time this great high priest represents God vis-à-vis humanity. In the name of God he confronts humanity and comes down to the level of humanity to speak God's word and to offer communion with God. Golgotha shows us the frightful result of this high-priestly mediation. The sum total of human aversion to God is now vented against him; the wellspring of hate against God, always alive in the human heart, is directed against him. The human race breaks all communion with God, banishes him from their lives, and pushes him away, crying, "We don't want him, we don't want him." And at the very moment that vain and hateful humanity throws off the yoke of God, Christ, too, suffers the darkness of God's abandonment. God also refuses him and pushes him away; God, too, lets him slide into the utter darkness of eternal night. The cross signifies abandonment in the most absolute sense of the word. God and humanity sing the same tune here in their conviction of this particular man, who functioned as a mediator between these two. The cross does not belong to the earth, nor does it accord with heaven. It cannot be counted to belong to earthly territory, but it doesn't fit in that other world either — the world of pure light and divine majesty. The cross is simply pure night, nothing but outright terror.

For a brief moment, the thought occurs to us that now the balance of the world is tipping over, that everything is up for grabs, that the future of creation in all its parts is in jeopardy. Suppose that the great mediator at that moment turns back to God, lets go of the human race, and pronounces the divine curse on that immense volume of human hate. Yes, he would save his own skin; yes, he would, at that moment, side with God against us humans. Then, from the cross, a terrible curse would descend over all human sin. And then this world would also drown into nothingness. Then creation would no longer have a purpose and all would be lost. Then we and our children could only look forward to doom and death.

There is still another possibility. What if the great mediator at that moment falls back on us humans, lets go of God, and starts a mighty revolt against God? Then, too, he would save his skin. He could be released from the cross because all cause of hatred on the part of the world would be removed — since he would be one of us. But that would also mean that, at that very moment, God would remove himself infinitely far away from us. This would mean that from then on, in the most perfect sense of the word, we would have to manage without God in the world.

If Jesus can no longer bear the great burden of brokenness, if he goes one way or the other, then the cross will be the eternal breaking point between God and humanity. The only option left for us at that time would be to be swallowed up in the deep night of death.

But if he does carry through, if he persists until the bitter end; if he remains our representative before God until death, and represents God before us; if he endures the searing pain to the point of being consumed — then there is salvation. This is impossible to imagine, and there are no words for it. Our minds cannot grasp this because here all human thinking stops. "What the eye has not seen, and the ear has not heard, and what has not welled up in a human heart, God has prepared." We see it, but we cannot fathom it. It is so totally mysterious, so impossibly grand and glorious, that we stand and gaze from afar. Something happened that cannot be expressed in any language; it cannot be grasped by the greatest minds in the world. This is the work of God. All we can do is honor God's holy plan of salvation and bow down before him in total adoration. Adam, the new Adam, went past the cherubim into paradise, went through death, his own death. And in him we all went through death as well — as he carried us with him — because we all are part of his body. This is not a historical fact in the common sense of the word, because it carries no expiration date: it is good forever. It belongs to the *Urzeit*, which gives meaning and shape to history, the basis of all that was and is and is to come. Everything that ever happened, from ancient times until the last day, rests on this one happening, which stands at the center of the great stream of history. One single fact emerges infinitely far above everything else, spanning all ages and tying *Urzeit* and end-time together: Golgotha, that is, the cross — that is, Jesus Christ.

Upon further reflection, we notice that, in this stage of the passion drama, everything has a double meaning: things are what they are, and simultaneously they are what they are not. Christ is God: he reveals God, and whoever sees him sees God; as such he is crucified by us. Christ is God, and we humans are humans. The cross is the expression of sin, the crime of paradise but now infinitely magnified and reinforced, projected in gigantic proportions onto the screen of eternity. However, that is not the ultimate meaning of the cross. Christ is human, is *adam*, the one burdened with sin. He is what he is not: the roaming exile outside paradise, he is humanity — he is all of us. And the people who nailed him to a cross — taking God's role and place, saying what God says, doing what God does — they are what they are not. The crucifixion is true in a double sense: all those who take part in this happening are both themselves and are different from themselves. All this makes these scenes so difficult to perceive and to understand at first glance. We put God on the cross and God puts us on the cross, and both actions converge: the two are one and the same event. That is why the cross is the most extreme result of sin, and at the same time a miracle of grace, so immeasurably great and beautiful that it is beyond our comprehension. Streams of grace flow from this event. This is the point where the universe is anchored.

The End

Jesus' death is followed by several signs that point, beyond any doubt, to the glory of him who had departed. "At this moment the curtain of the Temple was torn in two from top to bottom. The earth shook and the rocks split. The tombs broke open and the bodies of many holy people who had died were raised to life" (Matt. 27:51-52).

The tearing of the curtain in the Temple is a symbol of profound significance. The curtain, after all, closed off paradise and kept us from seeing it. It was the great secret of the Temple and belonged to its very essence. That Temple united within itself two aspects: God's proximity and his remoteness. God is always present in the midst of his people — he lives in Israel's center — and yet he is impossibly distant, never seen by human eye, impossible to be approached by any human ever. Only the high priest was allowed to enter, and then only once a year, as a symbolic indication of what one day would be reality. When that curtain tears, it means that the temple has lost its meaning. The earthly office of high priest is exposed as an empty ceremony, and the former service of shadows, which culminated with the high priest entering in the Holy of Holies, is stamped as a vain show. None of this makes sense anymore. The entire ritual has lost its value now that the great high priest has shed his blood in the outer courts of the world and is ready to enter into the eternal holy place.

At the same time, paradise now opens up. No more is the Holy of Holies accessible to only one person who may view the beauty of the cover of atonement and the cherubim looking down on it. The way is now open for all. In the one and only true high priest, all are included who belong to him, and everybody has free and open access to the throne of grace.

The Death of Humanity

Not only is the curtain torn at this point, but there is also an earthquake. It is at this juncture that nature and history meet. Nature, always a neutral observer of the dramatic happenings of human history, now edges closer and closer to what humans do and shares in the horror over what is happening on earth. Wars have been waged across the world, cities burned down, and genocides perpetrated. Untold mourning and sadness have been inflicted on humanity from time immemorial. Yet nature has remained unaffected and has not changed. Every year trees still bud, flowers still bloom, untouched by war or misery, as if there were no war, no injustice, no despair. (Translator's note: The reader should remember that Bavinck wrote the above in 1946, long before the concept of climate change was part of the popular consciousness.)

Nature is the background against which human history plays out. She remains unmoved amidst all the commotion, all the consternation. Nature and humans no longer recognize each other; they have become strangers ever since the mysterious link with the kingdom was broken and the entire creation was torn into shreds. But this one human being, Jesus, causes nature to react. Now that the true Adam fights his death struggle on Golgotha, now something miraculously new vibrates throughout nature: rocks crumble, atoms tremble, and the whole wide world shudders. This Adam comprised the entire creation. He carried the entire world on his strong shoulders. His death caused indescribable upheaval in all sectors of the universe.

THERE LIES GOLGOTHA. Soon dusk descends and the shadows of the night take over. Golgotha, the heart of the world, has revealed the ultimate truth, the truth about us humans and about God. This was the scene of the grand event that reunited heaven and earth again. Death and heaven were here, hideous darkness and luminous light, and sin and grace met here. All the strands of world history converged here, in the presence of God and his human creatures. The cross is the sole message of the Bible. Everything in it expresses the truth of the cross. Whoever has understood the cross has seen God.

CHAPTER 10

Born Again

Resurrection

For the third time the Bible takes us along to a garden, this time to the garden of Joseph of Arimathea. In the Garden of Eden, Adam dwelt in the first paradise, and he wanted to be equal to God; in the Garden of Gethsemane, God called to him, "Adam, where are you?" In the third garden we again are placed in paradise. The chapters in the Gospels that describe Jesus' suffering are closely connected to Genesis 3, a chapter that anticipates Matthew 26 and 27. While Genesis 1 and 2 tell us about the birth of creation, Matthew 28 indicates the start of the new creation, the beginning of the new heaven and the new earth, the morning of the new creation.

The ancient peoples of the East imagined the world as a perpetual cycle of regeneration. Their vision was that, from the height of the golden era, humanity slowly descends into a time when everything turns into chaos. But then light breaks through and a new world period emerges, leading to another golden age. Yet life again deteriorates — slowly but inexorably. Confusion and dissolution return, the powers of decay undermine human happiness, and the demise of all things once more occurs. That is how the world rushes on from one world period to the next, forever and ever.

Such is the cyclical, circular thinking of the ancient Orient. It took its cue from the natural cycle, the succession of day and night, of rise and fall, of life and death, and they applied this process to history, which they viewed as an enormously long day ending in the twilight of the evening. Then, from the night a new day is born, a day that nonetheless already contains the germ of darkness. At best, Hindu people, for example, made allowances for an escape from this cycle, an effort to place themselves outside this process by extricating themselves from the world via silent meditation. But no culture achieved a break from these philosophical positions that resulted in overcoming this cycle.

It is the distinctive feature of the Bible that it sees everything in its brute reality. Death is truly death; life is real life. This world is, indeed, subject to the doom of death, because humanity *(adam)* broke the meaningful context of the kingdom. But there is no cycle — only a continuation of a process, a steady progress from death to death, from doom to doom. But, in contrast to the negative, the Bible also knows the hymn of victory, the message of the resurrection. This resurrection is not a new birth that later leads to a new demise; it is not the start of a new cycle that once again will end in death. This resurrection is a break with death: it is "resurrection" in the total sense of the word. It is new creation — rebirth. Matthew 28 harks back to Genesis 1 and can only be compared to that opening chapter, which means that the Bible stands apart as a unique book, a book with a content that is entirely different from any other book in the world. The Bible did not come into being through "the will of man, but men spoke from God as they were carried along by the Holy Spirit" (2 Pet. 1:21).

Along this route the Bible takes us to Joseph of Arimathea's garden. It is remarkable that the Bible tells us so little about this garden. No Tree of Life at its center enters the picture, nor do we read about the Tree of the Knowledge of Good and Evil. The Bible does not mention the four rivers that flow from the garden and irrigate the life originating from God. Not a word does it devote to the animals, or to the birds of heaven that sing and warble in honor of their maker. This new paradise does not mention these things at all, nor does it emphasize the beauty of this garden, or the multitude of flowers or fruits. There is only the garden, paradise, and in that paradise there is only one person: Adam. It is Adam who has gone through death, has passed by the cherubim, and now has returned to the world, the place intended by God's counsel to be the dwelling place for humanity. The entire emphasis now is on that one human being.

Here the Bible goes all out to tell us that we are standing on the threshold of a new world. When, later, the book of Revelation describes for us in living color how the New Jerusalem comes down out of heaven, and how there, in that holy city, the rivers of life flow and the Tree of Life grows, all of that is the result of what happens here. Here the rebirth of all things finds its start; here the new world has its beginning. Here the morning stars again sing their joyous tune together, and all God's children and the holy angels shout for joy over the miracle that a new world has arisen (Job 38:7).

The good news of the resurrection sparkles with unparalleled brightness and joy; it is a pure ode to God. Small wonder that Paul, in his Letters, declares so emphatically, "More than that: he was raised to life" (Rom. 8:34). Christ has indeed been raised from the dead, the first fruits of those who have fallen asleep (1 Cor. 15:20). In the Revelation of John, Christ himself says to his astounded disciple: "Do not be afraid. I am the first and the last. I am the living one; I was dead, and behold I am alive forever and ever" (Rev. 1:17-18). Throughout the New Testament a melody of wonderful exuberance resonates over that Easter morning in the garden of Joseph of Arimathea. Here all things start anew; here lies the cradle of the new humanity, the start of a new future.

At first glance we are struck by the fact that the gospel of the resurrection lacks all the dramatic tensions that made the previous chapters so emotional. The happenings here no longer have a double function of simultaneously being what they are and what they are not. Here humanity is not God, and God is not expelled for being human. In the gospel of the resurrection, everything goes back to that wonderful clarity and openness that was so typical of the first chapters of the Bible. We have returned to the source of it all, and there is not a single muddy stream, not a single dissonance that throws a false note into the melodious symphony of God's wondrous works. In the new paradise there is only the one: Adam, that is, the second Adam, "the man come from heaven," the "life-giving spirit" (1 Cor. 15:46-47). And this "man from heaven" is who he is, no longer in the form of a servant, no longer having an appearance that does not fit with his new, highly exalted dignity.

It is also striking that nobody from elsewhere can approach him and set him in his place. We cannot tell him that we do not want him or will not accept him. We cannot treat him as if he is something other than what he is. We cannot arrest him again and convict him once more. We cannot even seek him out because we do not know where he is. He alone elects

Born Again

to whom he will appear as he seeks out the one and passes by the other. He takes up a relationship with those who belong to him, and none can relate to him of their own accord. He is the one in charge: everything proceeds from him. He is the only one who takes the initiative: all others must simply accept what he does. At one time he was the suffering one who had to endure what others did to him as he submitted to being a butt of jokes, being spit on, and being flogged. Now he is the one in charge, the only one who acts, while all others can only watch from a distance and submit to what pleases him.

Everything indicates that here we are dealing with an essential change: Christ has ceased to be self-emptying. He has become what he is. Until Golgotha he was the first Adam and carried the guilt and the death that afflicted humanity. His situation was outside paradise. His residence was the world; his destiny was death. But now, having passed through death, he has received new qualities. He now is the *ganz Andere*, the "wholly other." His place is now in paradise, his residence is next to God, and his destiny is life. He is now the one crowned with glory, the beatified one. Through death he has now entered paradise "by his own blood" (Heb. 9:12), and he has acquired his imperishable glory. He is now in paradise, he is the Tree of Life, and the rivers of life-giving waters spring from his throne (Rev. 22:1). In his visions Ezekiel had seen how a river of living water flowed out of the Holy of Holies in the temple toward the East (Ezek. 47). That inner holy place was paradise, the garden of Arimathea, and in that garden was Jesus.

Jesus rose from the dead on a spring morning when, in the distance, the day was dawning. A faint glimmer of light tried to penetrate the tall trees, and on the horizon purple streaks signaled the arrival of a new day. Birds twittered in the foliage, flowers began to unfold, and a general air of expectation spread throughout the garden. This was the morning of creation, the *Urzeit* when God saw all that he had made. This was also the end-time, the new world where justice dwelt. *Urzeit* and end-time came together in the garden of Joseph of Arimathea: Joseph's garden lay between the Garden of Eden and the New Jerusalem, bordering on both. Spanning all the centuries of world history, right here in the garden of Joseph, the first and the second paradise met each other. It was the birth of the new creation. He who stood here is the "alpha and the omega, the beginning and the end, the first and the last." *Urzeit* and end-time were next to each other and touched each other at one point — right here in the garden of Joseph. All those long and dramatic centuries of the world's history were nothing but a lightning flash past the garden.

The Appearances

In far greater detail than the sober account of the resurrection, the Gospels depict the several appearances of the risen Savior. These appearances take us back to the realm of history. They pull us out of the sphere of the *Urzeit*, where the unchangeable realities that are at the base of our very lives reside and get us in touch with the tremendous workings of world history in which God prepares the coming of his eternal kingdom. That means that we are at once ushered out of paradise again, to face the needs and doubts, the struggles and tensions, that are so typical of life in our historical situation.

It is impossible, in this limited space, to comment on every one of these appearances. We have to limit ourselves by drawing a few lines and by indicating some characteristic details. The first thing to note in these appearances is that they often show, in a variety of ways, that it truly is Jesus who appears. When Jesus met with his disciples, he showed them his hands and his side (John 20:20). He emphatically assured them: "Why are you troubled and why do doubts rise in your minds? Look at my hands and my feet. It is I myself! Touch me and see; a ghost has no flesh and bones as you see I have" (Luke 24:38-39). Jesus commanded Thomas to place his hand in Jesus' side (John 20:27) so that there would not be any doubting the fact that it really was Jesus. In that same vein, I should point out how often partaking of food is mentioned in the Gospels. Jesus breaks bread with the men on the way to Emmaus (Luke 24:30); in the full gathering of the disciples he takes a piece of fish to eat (Luke 24:41-43); and he and his disciples have breakfast together on the shore of the Sea of Tiberias (John 21:12-13). These repeated meals are meant as irrefutable indications that Jesus reappeared not as a ghost but was indeed raised from the dead with his own body. Eating is a sacrament: it indicates our affinity to the earth, and by eating we confess our unity with the earth. When Christ on several occasions after his resurrection ate meals in the company of his disciples, it is a clear indication that he still belonged to this world, that he maintained connection to this world and that he embraced it.

A second striking feature is that some appearances demonstrated a certain distance between the resurrected one and his disciples. This kind of distance was perfectly normal and obvious. They did not dare ask him any questions; they sat next to him on the beach silently, waiting to see if he was going to say anything (John 21:12). Jesus himself created distance when there was a risk that this distance was not fully understood. To a deeply moved Mary Magdalene, who in a worshiping pose tried to embrace him, he said: "Do not hold on to me, for I have not yet returned to the Father" (John 20:17). Appearing on the mountain in Galilee as the great king, he especially radiated a glow of elevated majesty that immediately pointed to the big difference between that time and the time before the crucifixion (Matt. 28:16-20). Jesus also would suddenly show up to a person or persons without prior notification. That they did not know where to look for him proved that he was different from before, that he belonged to another world system that could not be gauged by normal human criteria. His body, even though it had ties to the earth, was no longer subject to the natural laws of hunger and thirst, or to cold and heat, or to weight and inertia. It carried unmistakable signs of a higher order that far exceeds the normal terrestrial laws.

A third hallmark was the frequent reference to the spoken and written Word. Already at the first appearance to the women, the angel reminds them: "Remember how he told you, while he was still with you in Galilee . . ." (Luke 24:6). To the men on the road to Emmaus, Christ himself said: "How foolish you are, and how slow to believe all that the prophets have spoken!" (Luke 24:25). He assured the disciples that "everything must be fulfilled that is written about me in the Law of Moses, the Prophets and the Psalms" (Luke 24:44). At every meeting the risen master repeatedly pointed to Scripture about his appearances, because they were in their nature miraculous occurrences. The church was not to live by these events; it was not to feed on them, but on the Word that remains effective throughout the ages. "Blessed are those who have not seen and yet have believed" (John 20:29).

All this is closely connected to the continuous reminder of the mandate the disciples and the church after them have in this world. World history rushes on, and in that history the church has a heavy and solemn responsibility. "Therefore go and make disciples of all nations, baptizing them in the name of the Father and the Son and the Holy Spirit, and teaching them everything I have commanded you" (Matt. 28:19). "Go into all the world and preach the good news to all creation" (Mark 16:15). "You will be my witnesses in Jerusalem, and in all Judea and Samaria, and to the ends of the earth" (Acts 1:8). The band of disciples were to be deeply aware of their responsibility toward the world and the history of humanity. From now on, history's dominant theme for all ages to come is the kingdom of God and the coming of the kingdom. The church must stand in that world as a vital force. She may never — not even for a moment — abandon the world to its own devices. Rather, she must see the entire world as the territory where God intends to build his kingdom.

The disciples were of the opinion that, immediately after the resurrection, the end-time was imminent. They were convinced that, after the second Adam had risen from the dead, *Urzeit* and end-time flowed together, and God's mighty kingdom would reveal itself as a ready-made reality. Even as late as their climbing the mount of ascension, they still were asking: "Lord, are you at this time going to restore the kingdom to Israel?" By that kingdom they meant the commencement of the great kingdom that was to come through Israel (Acts 1:6). In this expectation they felt backed up by the prophets of the Old Testament, who always had the coming of the Messiah intimately connected with the glorious end-time, when God would unite the world under the royal auspices of the throne of David. Jesus wanted to show them that the first rays of the morning sun had indeed risen over the dawning of the end-time, but that the coming of that kingdom would still require an infinite amount of trouble and effort. The church herself would be mobilized for that purpose as the messenger of the salvation of the Lord, and she would fearlessly have to make her way through the world, always with her eye focused on the *telos*, the end that God would bring about before long.

What strikes us, finally, is that in these appearances Jesus associated himself with the disciples. They are together in this undertaking, as is evident from John 20:21: "As the Father has sent me, I send you." When they go out into the world to bring the good news, Christ accompanied them. "And surely I am with you always, to the very end of the age" (Matt. 28:20).

From now on, their message was to be his message; their need was his need; their struggle was his struggle. From now on Christ himself would be present in world events: he stands in the center of world history and rules as one to whom is given "all power in heaven and on earth" (Matt. 28:18). Christ and those who belong to him are one, and nobody can separate these two from each other. The disciples stood in the world in the place of Christ, and in them and through them Christ reached out to the nations of the world.

This last thought is the motif of the book of the Bible that we have given the title Acts of the Apostles. In the apostles' acts it is Christ who is the only subject, the only actor: he takes the initiative, he preaches, and he does the miracles. Actually, what are told to us in this book are much more "the acts of the risen Christ." When Philip goes to Samaria, it is really Christ who goes there; when Peter enters the house of Cornelius, it is really Christ who personally pays a visit there; and when Paul travels to Lystra and Derbe, to Athens and Corinth, and even to Rome, the apostles are Christ's feet that walk through those cities of Asia and Europe. The total unity, in spirit and in body, of the church with the Lord is the background of everything we are told about the early church.

"In Christ"

In many of his Letters, the apostle Paul uses the short expression "in Christ." No fewer than 164 times he writes either "in Christ" or "in the Lord," proof positive that this is what drives his entire outlook. When we wonder what he means by this phrase, it is naturally necessary to compare the different passages with each other and thus to arrive at a more comprehensive conclusion. An analysis makes it apparent that that the words "in Christ" have five different facets.

1. In the first place, this expression and those of a similar nature point to a special, intimate *relationship* that developed between Christ and his followers. Paul directs his greetings to those "who are in the Lord" (Rom. 16:11); he knows there is no damnation "for those who are in Christ Jesus" (Rom. 8:1). To be "in Christ" means to be his possession, to belong to him in life and in death.

2. In the second place, this formula is also used to signify that a certain situation or a certain way of action is closely related to the *work of Christ*. When Paul came to preach in Troas, a door was opened "in the Lord" (2 Cor. 2:12), meaning that Christ was at work there. We can "walk in him" (Col. 2:6); we can "speak the truth in Christ" (Rom. 9:1); the congregation in Rome must accept Phoebe "in the Lord" (Rom. 16:2). All these acts, done in Christ, share something of his light, are permeated with his spirit, and are carried by his love.

3. The phrase "in Christ" is also used particularly in the several sayings that express appreciation for what the *servants of Christ* have done or have said. Apelles is tested and approved in Christ (Rom. 16:10); the members of Corinth were "mere infants in Christ" (1 Cor. 3:1). In that vein, Paul intends for all his pupils to be "perfect in Christ" (Col. 1:28).

4. This mode of speech is also found in many places where it concerns the *objective salvation* that God has prepared for us. Paul says to Timothy that he must "be strong in the grace that is in Christ Jesus" (2 Tim. 2:1); the love of God is "in Christ Jesus" (Rom. 8:39); our salvation we have "in him" (Eph. 1:7); the promise of God is "in Christ Jesus" (Eph. 3:6); we are "justified in Christ" (Gal. 2:17); we are made alive "in Christ" (1 Cor. 15:22); and we have freedom "in Christ Jesus" (Gal. 2:4).

5. In the last place, the phrase "in Christ" has a *cosmic, all-encompassing* meaning. We all are "one body in Christ" (Rom. 12:5); "in him the whole building is joined together and rises to become a holy temple" (Eph. 2:21); "in him all things hold together" (Col. 1:17); "he purposed in Christ, to be put into effect when the time has reached its fulfillment, to bring all things together in heaven and on earth under one head, even Christ" (Eph. 1:9-10). In Christ peace is made between Jew and Gentile; indeed, the entire world is brought back to the unity in which God had created it (Eph. 2:15).

This last example goes back to the basis of the worldview that we so often encounter in the New Testament. Everything in this world is either in Adam or in Christ. Everything that is in Adam carries the symptoms of the life of Adam and finds its motivation in the powers that motivated Adam. To be in Adam means to be outside paradise, to be an exile fleeing before the flaming swords of the cherubim, to worship the earth that now is Adam's sole possession, to be small and vulnerable and yet to think of oneself as a god who can determine his own path according to his own desires. Whoever is in Adam is also *adam*, a creature walking around with the false notion of his own divinity, promoting his own ideas as norm for everything. Whoever is in Adam has in his innermost being a primal fear of God, a result of his flight into darkness. Whoever is in Adam lives under the eternal threat of judgment. Whoever is in Adam has broken out of the kingdom, has become a solitary figure in creation, one who no longer understands the meaning of the world — while the world no longer understands him. Those who are in Adam are cobuilders of the kingdom of humanity, the Tower of Babel, in which the disintegrating and fragmented human race repeatedly tries to rediscover unity. Over against this "in Adam" is that overwhelming reality of being "in Christ." Those who are in Christ have passed through doom and death, are back in paradise, are in the meaningful context of the eternal kingdom of God; they are released from all fear and stand with head upright, waiting for the glorious revelation of the Lord's salvation that is to come (see 1 Cor. 15:45-49).

Seen in that light, the short phrase "in Christ" is infinitely rich in content. It refers back to the eternal, divine decree that God "chose us in him before the creation of the world" (Eph. 1:4). With that decree God made us part of Christ, regards us as one with Christ, includes us in him. And on that decree rests our salvation, our redemption from the clutches of this toilsome world.

Seen from that perspective, the expression "in Christ" has the meaning of a worldwide, cosmic life bond. Whoever is included in that bond is one with Christ: that is, everything that happens to Christ also happens to them. They are "united with him like this in his death" (Rom. 6:5); they are "buried with him through baptism into death" (Rom. 6:4); they are "raised up with Christ" and are "with him in the heavenly realms" (Eph. 2:6). Whatever is in Christ is also in them: they are no longer what they are, but they are what Christ is. They have even gone through death into God's paradise, which is nothing other than the kingdom in its glorious manifestation. When Adam destroyed paradise, paradise retreated to heaven, even though it remained on earth in the temple as a reminder that made paradise a living reality. It is in that paradise that those who are "in Christ" are included. They are with Christ in that paradise. Their residence is that paradise: their *politeuma* ("citizenship") is in the heavens (Phil. 3:20). These people no longer belong to the world that has surrendered itself to the powers of destruction, and they no longer are part of this age, this particular period of the world. They are in intimate contact with the coming age, the period of the radiant, divine light. Everything is so new in Christ that Paul lacks the ability to put this newness into words strong enough to reflect this reality: "If anyone is in Christ, he is a new creation; the old has gone, the new is come" (2 Cor. 5:17). The old world, named after Adam, has disappeared under our feet, and the new world has begun in Christ Jesus. Christ and Adam are the two who stand opposite each other in this world — as the new and the old, as heaven and earth (1 Cor. 15:49). It is the most radical contrast imaginable.

And yet Christ did stand where Adam stood: outside paradise. Christ started his redemptive work at the place where Adam went under. But Christ took up and pursued the rescue operation until it attained the full glory of God. When this universe was about to perish, Christ prevented it from going under and rescued it. He has placed all things in a redemptive relationship to God, "whether things on earth or things in heaven" (Col. 1:20).

That is why the expression "in Christ" is an indication of a new cosmic life situation. Those who are in Christ find themselves in the harmonious context of the new world, and they share in everything that is in Christ, not only in his death but no less in his resurrection, not only in his ascension but no less in his dwelling in eternal nearness to the Father. To be in Christ means to breathe the atmosphere of the new world, to live, to think, to suffer, to act out of a new life principle, aimed at the coming age, when Christ will surrender his kingdom to the Father so that God will be all and in all.

Because the bond of being "in Christ" is of such dominating significance in Scripture, we can understand why the earliest theologians tried to find ways to express this bond in a more or less logical way. They wished to see it as a mystical melding with Christ. Closer analysis, however, shows that it is not correct to consider being in Christ a mystical experience. Being in Christ has nothing to do with mystical ecstasy, with spiritualizing, with emotionalism, with being in the seventh heaven. It's true that those who are "in Christ" no longer live for themselves, but Christ lives in them; on the other hand, they are still fully responsible for the world and exist there fully aware of what is going on. There is nothing unreal about this, nothing of an otherworldly mysticism. No, being "in Christ" is of a wholly other order entirely — deeper and more mysterious, even sober, pragmatic, and down to earth. It is not something that human understanding can grasp, nor can it be expressed in words or compared to any single human relationship. Perhaps it can best be pictured as an ocean liner that plows her way through immense seas. Only those who are "in" the vessel, who experience every movement of that ship, who are carried along with her, are safe, free from the world of drowning death that threatens them on every side. But even that metaphor does not go very far in expressing the unsearchable riches of what it means to be in Christ.

The Coming Age

This world, carrying the stamp of Adam, is rushing toward its demise. The forces of dissolution and confusion are accelerating as the forces of decay become more evident from year to year. There is the spirit of lawlessness at work, the breaking up of the world order that covertly but energetically undermines human history. There are still powers at work that keep that mysterious process in check and prevent it from coming totally out in the open. But once this restraining force ceases, the "mystery of iniquity" will emerge with unbridled power. Then "the man of sin, the son of perdition," the "enemy," will sit down in God's temple and proclaim himself to be God (2 Thess. 2:3-8). That person is Adam, who is the ultimate destiny of those who are "in Adam."

Straight through the frightening appearance of the Antichrist, the new age will be realized, when Christ will emerge as the victor. The Revelation of John depicts this final victory in a series of breathtaking scenes. The demonic powers that have operated undercover for so long will seek an outlet and will reveal themselves in the horrible scenarios of the endtime. This world is being readied for self-destruction, as it hastens with indomitable force toward the end. It is rushing on from darkness to darkness, until the light of Christ breaks through, until the new heaven and the new earth are born, where all ruptures will be healed and where the light of the kingdom of God that has come *in Christ* will shine eternally and gloriously.

CHAPTER 11

The Road to Life

In Adam — In Christ

One of the greatest thoughts the Bible teaches us is that we humans, as we appear in history, always portray somebody. We are either in Adam or we are in Christ. We can never stand by ourselves as creatures that can determine our lives on our own, of our own free will. We always stand in a wide cosmic connection, are always included in an all-encompassing relationship.

Born into this world, we are by nature "in Adam." That means we are rooted in this cosmic context that is Adam's hallmark. His place is outside paradise; his attitude is one of primeval fear of God, evident in his flight from the flaming sword; his habitat is this world; and his destiny is the curse and death. Being "in Adam" also means that what is so striking about Adam is also typical of us. We are always eating from the Tree of the Knowledge of Good and Evil, that is, we are always trying to determine on our own what is good and what is not — according to our own norms and our needs. We are always busy promoting our own divinity and centering our lives on our own interests. We are always busy shying away from our responsibilities and trying to hide when that loud "Adam, where are you?" resonates in our ears. We are always trying to find excuses for our shortcomings and to blame others — the world, even God. In short, we are always *adam:* we have *adam* features grafted into the core of our being. It is not true that each of us at a given moment entered the world as a new creature. No, from birth we stand in a relationship: we are *adam*, and all we do and think is related to our being *adam*. We have constructed our impressive pyramids, we have reclaimed land, rerouted rivers, established empires, carved beautiful images of gods out of the rocks, composed wonderful poetry such as the *Divine Comedy, Hamlet,* and *Faust,* have painted the *Night Watch,* and have written the *Critique of Pure Reason.* But in all this we remain in *adam,* that is, we remain human. We have never succeeded in escaping that fatal flaw that is ours from the day of our birth. Humanity — all of us — remains caught up in a cosmic life-relationship that forever remains an enigma for us.

We might perhaps explain this cosmic connection by pointing to our blood relationship. Via our bloodlines we are, from a genealogical perspective, tied to our ancestors because we do not come into the world as something entirely different, something new: from day one, we are part of what our forefathers have done and undergone. In addition, we need not merely point to inherited traits that play a role in determining our future, but also to the important value of tradition, which has shaped us from our earliest years. Considering these factors, we could say that we all are part of a cosmic life condition and connected through genealogy with all previous blood relatives.

By itself, there is some justification for using this blood relationship to understand and explain ourselves as participants in this cosmic life condition. The Bible, too, points to the physical relationship as a factor that unites all people. Still, this is not usually the way the Bible expresses itself. Rather than emphasize the blood connection, the Bible uses the much more meaningful word "covenant" to characterize the intimate relationship between people in general. *Covenant* always has a theological aspect because it is connected to God. The blood relationship can be seen as purely belonging to this world, apart from God, thus outside the divine realm. But the word "covenant" indicates from the very first a connection to God as its most decisive feature. God regards all people as participants in that one covenant of which Adam was the head. In Adam all people have broken the covenant with God. There is a covenant connection between humanity and God, and this relationship supposes and guarantees the unity of all of the world's people. It's true that every human being, as soon as he or she sees the light of day, stands before God as a human being, as *adam,* as a fugitive banished from paradise, and as an exile from God's kingdom. That is "the human" in all humans. In every other respect, we can differ substantially: some are rich, some poor; some belong to the most primitive tribes, others have the advantage of a long history of science; some lack brainpower or are mentally deficient, while others are blessed with extraordinary talents, capable of major accomplishments. We can differ in ever so many ways, but what we all have in common is that we are all *adam*.

It is self-evident that the *adam* characteristics manifest themselves differently in our individual lives. Some try to assert themselves as gods through brute egoism: rough and tough, they attempt to claim all within their grasp. Others see themselves as unrecognized geniuses, misunderstood victims of a cruel and insensitive world. Some revel in visionary moods as they pursue occult ways to become one with a Universal Spirit and to lose themselves in the sphere of the divine; others live a life of pious virtue and try to keep up their self-respect by any means possible. We are all different, but in one respect we are all the same: our ineradicable desire to be autonomous, to be ourselves, to take charge of our own lives. We all are little "gods," even if we all have different ways of showing it. World history unfolds in a sphere of differentiation, but all this dissimilarity suffers irrevocably from the unalterable reality of being *adam*.

This undeniable fact also implies that it is impossible for us humans to escape being *adam*. We cannot free ourselves from the unbreakable tie with that cosmic connection that dominates us from cradle to grave. We are "in Adam" and cannot break free from it, simply because outside Adam there is no point where we can stand. We simply cannot pull ourselves free from the suction power of the connection that is indicated by the name Adam. We can never be strictly ourselves, a new creature, a tabula rasa, a blank piece of paper. That is the hopelessness of all human existence, because, in spite of all our efforts, we humans are and will remain "in Adam" till our last breath.

That compelling cosmic connection that I have given the title "in Adam" cannot be broken until we humans enter the sphere of influence of a different and new connection that is more powerful than the former. Jesus himself has expressed this in a parable in these words: "When a strong man, fully armed, guards his own house, his possessions are safe. But when someone stronger attacks and overpowers him, he takes away the armor in which the man trusted and divides up the spoils" (Luke 11:21-22).

If we, residing "in Adam" and abiding in the large, cosmic connection, are not able to extricate ourselves, we can only be rescued if there is another who is stronger than Adam. That is why there is only one escape route: we can only cease to be in Adam when we are in Christ. To be in Christ means to be incorporated again in the meaningful context of God's kingdom and to take up our position again next to the Tree of Life.

A New Creature

It needs no further comment that Scripture often mentions the border zone between what is "in Adam" and what is "in Christ." After all, that area is of the utmost importance for us in the daily struggle of life. In the preceding chapter I pointed out that here, too, Scripture maintains a theological point of view: that is, it strongly emphasizes that God is again the only one who takes the initiative, that he is the great Creator. He "chose us in him before the creation of the world" (Eph. 1:4). "For those God foreknew he also predestined to be conformed to the likeness of the Son" (Rom. 8:29). In other words, our being in Christ depends on the creating and redeeming will of God and is founded only on his grace and favor.

This does not alter the fact that, in our transition from the Adam connection to the Christ connection, our own will and our personal responsibility play a significant role. We may even express that as follows: the divine initiative to save us is realized in our life through our own decisions and our personal accountability. At work here is a wonderful divine interaction with our action and an equally miraculous inclusion of our will and action in the will and action of God himself, something we simply cannot unravel and thus must leave with him in his serene majesty. The main thing is that the transition from death to life does not come over us like something outside of our will, but that it is in part also *our* action, so that God's action is powerfully present in what *we* do.

That transition itself appears in Scripture under different names: sometimes it is described as coming to faith, or arriving at the truth, or sometimes as turning from one's ways, or being "delivered from the power of darkness and translated into the kingdom of the Son of God's love." The most significant is the concept of conversion, of turning from one's ways, of being born again, of repentance and renewal — terms that appear in numerous places in the New Testament. The word "renewal" signifies not a partial life-change but something far more: it means a relinquishing of the former connection with Adam and an assuming of a totally new connection with Christ Jesus. Renewal is a factual dying and being born again as a "new creature," a transition from one particular world to another. The only place in the three synoptic Gospels where the word "renewal" appears (Matt. 19:28: "the renewal of all things") points to the end-time, and hence possesses a marked eschatological orientation. Our very nature is connected to the *Urzeit* and what happened there, and that is the source of the inner strength in our lives. But through "renewal" we are directed toward the end-time, to the new age, the new time period in which Christ will be Lord. Renewal wrests us free from the Adam connection and places us in an intimate connection with Jesus Christ, who rose from death unto life.

That kind of renewal, with all its gifts and powers, makes up the whole person and affects him or her to the very core of his or her being. Renewal is a passage through the narrow gate, is a losing of oneself, a total self-abnegation, and an acknowledging in all humility of the unfathomable debt caused by our sinning. It is penance, self-examination leading to self-knowledge, and a going back as a humble child to the throne of the Father whom we have forsaken. Renewal includes a change in our very thinking, a *metanoia*. It is at the same time, however, a complete change in the totality of our conduct of life, a real desire of wanting to change and implementing that change. But all this does not show up as a valiant effort on our part to free ourselves from Adam's yoke but as a confession that we can do all this only through Christ — by being in him. It is exactly that kind of renewal that brings us into contact with Christ in the closest way possible, since this renewal is only conceivable through that contact. "He saved us through the washing of rebirth and renewal by the Holy Spirit, whom he poured out on us generously through Jesus Christ our Savior" (Titus 3:5-6). "He has given us new birth into a living hope through the resurrection of Jesus Christ from the dead" (1 Pet. 1:3). "If we have been united with him like this in his death, we will certainly also be united with him in his resurrection" (Rom. 6:5). Therefore, renewal is by its very nature nothing other than allowing our life-giving bond to Christ to take root in us and create a growing awareness of what his death and resurrection mean for us in the daily practice of our lives. We are "in Christ," and hence have died with him and have risen in him. Through renewal we now have a different perspective, a different residence: we stand in a different life situation that leads to a new lifestyle.

Baptism is the visible sign of renewal: it is the "bath of renewal" (in older translations, a "washing of regeneration" [Titus 3:5]). That baptism itself is a submerging in water, a "being buried with him through baptism into death" (Rom. 6:4); but at the same time it is a rising from death into newness of life. Via baptism we are taken up in that new life situation that is in Christ Jesus: we are grafted into him, we become branches of the vine that is Christ and thus become members of his body. No words can fathom that holy bond that through renewal has, in baptism, become part of our lives. It signifies our bond with the one who took Adam's place and through his death opened for us the way to the Tree of Life.

With a degree of nostalgia we recall how in the ancient church baptism was experienced as real renewal. Coming out of a pagan culture and the enchantments that life offered in it, people would hesitantly draw near to the cross of Jesus Christ, where they would gradually be taken in by his word, which displayed a new life in which only Christ was lord and king. At last, when such persons, drawn from darkness, experienced baptism, a new world would open up for them. That meant that they would often be shunned by their old friends, perhaps even their own parents, but they would be received in a new circle, the church of Christ, and they would stand with that church in the life-connection of the risen Savior. In the most perfect sense, that was real renewal, since the old was indeed a matter of the past, and behold, all had become new! In its ultimate sense, the fact of baptism can only be compared to the Flood, which had once consumed the ancient world, of which baptism was the contrast, the antitype (1 Pet. 3:21).

As it was then, so it is now: through baptism an old world, destined for destruction, was drowned forever, and a new world, one filled with God's precious promises, came to be. Baptism meant forsaking the world and becoming a new person for the sake of Christ. It was submerging in Christ and again rising in him. Baptism was the entrance to a new world, a new heaven and a new earth. It was customary during an earlier era to assume a new name to show once and for all that the old person was dead and a new one was born in Christ. That is how radically people experienced the transition from the old to the new, from Adam to Christ: "The old has gone, the new has come!" (2 Cor. 5:17).

In Two Different Life Relationships

Those who are born again, who have assumed a new name, suddenly find themselves in an extremely perilous situation. They are now "in Christ," in a different life situation; but it also means that they now live in this world under immense pressure. The battle has not yet been won; on the contrary, it now starts in earnest on all fronts.

In the first place, these born-again people still live in the midst of a world that lives out of Adam, a world that lives under the full control of the evil one (1 John 5:19). That means that they dwell, day in and day out, in a society that is in its entirety still under the curse from the *Urzeit* and in which demonic powers are still constantly at work — since they have taken possession of this world. The mighty current of life around them pushes with irresistible force in the direction of disintegration. Born-again Christians are standing in the middle of it and feel its suction power hour by hour.

In the second place, these born-again people also find themselves surrounded by secular life as it plays out in their immediate environment. Their very own country may be driven by tendencies to create a kingdom of humanity, a desire that has governed the national life of all peoples throughout the centuries. These attempts at establishing human empires can sometimes take the form of extreme measures, able to awaken imperial ambitions that can lead to great wars. All such wars display the desire to initiate large global empires, an aim that has fascinated the world's nations throughout the ages. These nations will try, at the same time, to mobilize all forces, to make all the powers of science and technology serve to promote national grandeur. To accomplish this, they will not tolerate internal discord, and they will punish any life that promotes different principles. Amid these circumstances, life for those who are "in Christ" will be extremely precarious, as they will feel threatened from all sides.

In the third place, these new converts — and all Christians — stand

The Road to Life

in the midst of world history, on the long road between *Urzeit* and endtime. History is shaped and governed by the forces that had their birth in the *Urzeit*. All of the world's history is a dramatically moving entity in which not only the different efforts to arrive at the formation of the human kingdom work at cross-purposes from each other, but also where all these attempts together collide with the mighty acts of God to prepare the coming of his eternal kingdom. World history is at the same time the history of human culture, which is the development of the capacities that abound in nature around us and are also present in our own minds. Art and science, music and literature, philosophy and technology, they all are just so many expressions of the ineradicable human desire to exploit their talents to the utmost and to make them useful for the greater human ideal. In the whole of human culture, even in its most noble expressions, it is *adam* — humanity personified, the one banished from paradise, the one chained to primeval fear — who is the engine and the prime mover. It all centers on the human being, concerned only with what humanity can accomplish, with what humans can achieve, with their potential and their creative ability. And it is in such a world, in world history with all its critical periods, that people stand who no longer are in *adam* but who are in Christ. They stand there as total strangers. They have escaped the enticements of the *Urzeit* and are now part of the new age, the new world — that is, they already live in the end-time. They are part of that hour that Jesus had in mind when he said, "A time is coming and has now come when the dead will hear the voice of the Son of God and those who hear will live" (John 5:25). That mysterious hour, which is coming but is now, which is always coming and always is — that is the atmosphere in which these people stand and breathe. They can already taste "the powers of the coming age" (Heb. 6:5).

We do not stand there all by ourselves, on our own. No, we are included in the great context of the church, "which is his body, the fullness of him who fills everything in every way" (Eph. 1:23). In the overall scheme of the world's population and of the history of the world, the church occupies a most remarkable place. In the ultimate sense, the church is outside the world, not included in the greater context of the world, because the world finds it origin outside paradise and intends to promote that frightful human kingdom, the kingdom of the Antichrist. In her essence the church is a peculiar phenomenon in the field of world events. She can never participate when the world wants to act in a united way, because she answers to the Other, because she lives with a different mindset. Nevertheless, the church has to state her position in an active and positive way, lest at some time or other she might fail in her responsibility.

However, the church can state her position in this world in several ways; indeed, in the course of her history she has done so repeatedly. In the first place, the church can withdraw from the world and give it over to the demons active in it. She can assume her distance from the world, lead her own life, far from the tumult of the nations and far from the culture wars. As a rule, the church can maintain such an ascetic attitude for only a short time; sooner or later she will be drawn back into the world, persecuted, vilified, and borne away again on the roaring river of world events.

In the second place, the church may seek to build an empire and try to impose God's kingdom on the world she inhabits. She can try to order that world and its institutions according to ideas shown in Scripture and thus attempt to transform the empires of her day into road signs of the great kingdom to come. The church can only do all these things when she has acquired a powerful position in a given territory, a position of strength that she must maintain at any price if she is not to fail miserably in her ambition. The Middle Ages were an example of such a striving for a Christian commonwealth in which the church was the leading power. In modern times, too, we encounter a number of examples that point in the same direction. The church wants to be a reforming and regenerating influence in the life of the world, in the arena of politics, in labor relations, with the aim that the life of the world might more and more reflect the kingdom of Christ.

In the third place, the church can, through its missionary efforts, aim to win the world for the gospel of Jesus Christ. She does this through being engaged both in purposeful organized missionary activity and through the simple preaching of each of her members. The early church, having next to no influence on the life of the world as a whole, displayed her vitality through the spontaneous witness of all of her members, and she indeed succeeded in a relatively short time to permeate the entire ancient world with the message of Christ. However, episodes of that kind of missionary effort are very rare in the life of the church.

The Road to Life

With all these different approaches, the church continually runs the grave and ever-present danger of being taken over by the world. The spirit of the world, originating from the principles of the *Urzeit*, is so overwhelmingly powerful that it threatens the church at every moment of her existence. This *Urzeit* spirit penetrates all her pores, makes her one with the world in her efforts to reform it, insinuates itself into her message. There have been times in the life of the church when she almost totally succumbed to the powers of the world, poisoned by the hardy germs that stem from the cosmic connection associated with Adam and drive history onward. During those times the simple faith in Christ sank away, and the church cooperated in the heroic efforts to realize the human kingdom here on earth. Those were the darkest days in the history of the church. Persecution is not a bad thing, but world conformity is: it is exactly what threatens us every day.

From all these different approaches, the church always falls back on her great longing for the end-time. Again and again, as if driven by unseen forces, the church remembers that she is not of this world, that she belongs to the coming age, and that she must aim all her efforts in that direction. This keen awareness of the end-time, this eschatological consciousness, is undergoing a strong revival throughout the church of Christ today. The terrible blows of two world wars in the twentieth century that lie behind us, the ruin of countless irreplaceable cultural treasures — they all remind us that we live in a world that is headed for destruction. The early church understood this, as is evident from the writings of that period. In the *Didachē*, one of the oldest writings of the early church, the prayer for the Lord's Supper went like this: *"Let grace abound, and let this world pass away. Maranatha!"* It is true that the church can witness the destruction of world cities, and in the shattering of all these treasures she senses that these horrendous human happenings will cause this terrible world to perish on account of the forces at work within it. The church experiences something of the jubilation of the redeemed in heaven when Babylon falls, when all the merchants of the world are in mourning over the big city and the saints in heaven call out to each other: "Rejoice over her, O heaven! Rejoice, saints and apostles and prophets! God has judged her for the way she treated you" (Rev. 18:20). This is not a perverse longing for death; this is a genuine conviction that this world is hastening toward destruction and that the grace of our Lord Jesus Christ will come via that destruction.

In the meantime, and in light of the above, it is sufficiently clear that it is not easy to explain in a few words what the place of the church might be in the overall perspective of life in this world. The best way to characterize the church's position is by contrasting the concepts of separation and compassion. The church can only separate herself from the world; she stands apart because she is rooted in a different soil than is the human race and belongs to a different age. Yet she may never be indifferent to the plight of the world, nor may she treat the world with disdain or lack of concern. The church can never abandon the world, never let go of her, because until the very end she sees the world as the territory of God's infinite possibilities. God is able to perform great miracles in that fallen world, and God can still involve many in the world in the plan he has for the redemption of the world. In that redemption plan the church herself is an instrument in God's hand: "As the Father has sent me, so I send you."

Those are the two poles between which the life of the church moves. She can only be fully engaged in the plight of the world when she knows enough to be "different" from the world, when she is keenly aware of the knowledge "that we are children of God, but that the whole world is under the control of the evil one" (1 John 5:19). Only when she is rooted in that knowledge can the church engage the world with unflagging energy. That knowledge also determines her relationship to national life — to culture and to history. But every time the church, moved by the needs of the world, starts to be busy there, she simultaneously feels the attraction emanating from the world, and she is pulled along, step by step, by the vital impulses that motivate the world. The church, in her history, has repeatedly had to be summoned to turn back from the world and to rediscover the separateness that determines her essence. It is the summons that is so succinctly formulated in the book of Revelation: "Come out of her, my people, so that you will not share in her sins, so that you will not receive any of her plagues" (Rev. 18:4). In the present dispensation, the church can never relax: her situation in the world is always precarious and always critical. To be caught between the two poles of her life situation is the cross that she must carry until the end of time.

The Road to Life

Crisis in One's Personal Life

In the personal life of the Christian, living in the world can lead to extremely difficult conflicts. These struggles are briefly pointed out in Scripture, which reminds us that Christians, even when they are born again and are in Christ (meaning that their residence is already in paradise), must daily cope with the powerful forces that still pulsate through their lives, which originate from the old Adam principle. Although those who are in Christ are in essence "translated" (Col. 1:13, KJV) from the power of darkness, that darkness still has a strong and durable influence over their thoughts and desires. They still always have to struggle with *adam*, with the "old self that is being corrupted by its deceitful desires" (Eph. 4:22). That concept of "the old self" is one of the typical observations in Paul's letters: it occurs on numerous occasions, and each time in a different way. In Romans 6:6 we read that "our old self was crucified with him so that the body of sin might be done away with, that we should no longer be slaves to sin." In Colossians 3:9, Paul appeals to the fact that "you have taken off your old self with its practices and have put on the new self." In Ephesians 4:22 we are cautioned "to put off [our] old self." Thus we are successively told that Christ's crucifixion also crucified our *adam*, and that we are also liberated from the powers of death; furthermore, we have rid ourselves of this *adam* the same way that we take off our coat; and finally, we are encouraged to continuously rid ourselves of the old self so that it not gain power over us again. That has been done already, but it has to be done again and again. In his death on the cross, Christ killed the old self in us, but it constantly wants to reassert itself and infect our lives anew. That primeval, cosmic connection "in Adam" is so unbelievably tough and persistent that every day anew it wants to sprout new forms.

That is "the old self." In other places the apostle uses the word "flesh" for the same idea, a remarkable instance of word usage in the Bible. "Flesh" is never merely an indication of our sensuous human nature; it always points to something deeper. In the Old Testament it points, as a rule, to the fragility and transitory nature of the human being, while in the New Testament it always indicates our affinity to the cosmic connection that is in Adam. We humans are outside paradise: we are exiles, we stand condemned, and our preferences incline toward the material world

— all that is included in the word "flesh." "I am flesh," the apostle laments, and he adds that he is "sold as a slave to sin" (Rom. 7:14). This means that, according to our natural life, we are always tied to that life situation into which we are all born with innumerable threads. "Flesh," or "the old self," is not dead matter; rather, it is a dynamic principle, a power that "makes me a prisoner of the law of sin" (Rom. 7:23). I am and will remain *adam* even though I am "in Christ." One moment I may exclaim that my "former self" and my *adam* have been crucified in Christ, and the next moment I discover that this same *adam* keeps me as a prisoner of war behind barbed wire and cruelly terrorizes me in my destitute condition. "What a wretched man I am! Who will rescue me from this body of death?" (Rom. 7:24). In that heart-rending cry Paul thoroughly exposes the duality of the Christian life.

It is true that we must put off the former self as a garment. Here, too, it is striking that the people of the Ancient Near East, as we have seen earlier, experience the link between themselves and their clothing in a much more intimate way than we do. They see their clothing as an expression of their personality, even an expression of the kind of mood they may be in. In that society clothing signifies persons: it reveals something of their very being and their authority. Clothing of that kind is not easily removed: it has to be torn off by force, which means that one has to become a different person, to become someone he or she is not. In the same way, we Christians have to get rid of the old self, which means that we must tear ourselves away from the dominating life situation typical of being in Adam. It means that we must cease to be rebels, must no longer desire to be like God or long to eat from the Tree of the Knowledge of Good and Evil. It also implies that we must no longer hide from God, compelled by the fear that is so deeply embedded in us. We must also cease to accuse others of our sins. In short, we must free ourselves from our human nature, from the *adam* in all of us, and clothe ourselves in that "new" humanity.

By the term "new humanity" Paul means nothing other than Christ himself. This is quite clear from Romans 13:14, where we read, "Rather, clothe yourselves with Jesus Christ." We must want to be more and more "in Christ," to live in that new life connection that appeared in him, die in his death and rise in his resurrection. We must abandon the old self, which means that we must do away with our sinful nature and become a different self. To become a different self means that we must become what in the deepest sense we already are: we are already in Christ, and it must be our utmost desire to be in Christ.

All this shows that, as it now stands, we have to deal with a host of paradoxes. We are in Christ while at the same time we are still in Adam; we are still flesh, sold into sin, rooted in the old life situation, and with all our power anchored in this world. We still belong to the earth, and yet our citizenship is in heaven; we still always secretly desire to have equality with God, and yet we have a part in him "who did not consider equality with God something to be grasped" (Phil. 2:6). We stand outside paradise as exiles, and yet we stand in Christ in the midst of it; we are driven by our great fear of the flaming sword, and yet we know that the cherubim long ago have sheathed their swords and now, full of expectation, they gaze at the cross. We are surrounded by paradoxes. We still belong to the present age, but we can already taste the powers of the coming age, and we know at the bottom of our hearts that it is there that we belong. We are still shouldering the curse of the *Urzeit*, and yet we know that this spell was broken on the cross and that we now look toward the end-time, the new paradise, the eternal and magnificent kingdom of our Lord Jesus Christ.

Urzeit and End-Time

We humans, as we live in the world, find ourselves in history; yet, at the same time, we are part of the imperishable and unchangeable forces that determine human life. We live in history, which means that we are at a certain juncture on the enormously long road of the major world events. These events rush over us, push through us, and dominate us every step of the way. As humans in history we cannot be compared with those of earlier generations, because we are different, we have our own peculiarities, and our existence now is typical of this moment of human history. But at the same time we are human, just as earlier generations were human and were also in Adam. The concept of being human has a great deal of baggage; its meaning derives from the *Urzeit*. In that concept there are still very faint memories of being created in God's image, but these recollections have been pushed away by the false notion that we are equal to God and have been concealed by our denial of the curse that was its consequence: that is, to be human means to belong to that powerful connection in Adam that, with never-flagging energy, strives to coordinate all powers to promote the human kingdom. Every human being born in this world is burdened with the primeval values contained in the concept of being human.

To be human means to stand between *Urzeit* and end-time. The road between these two extremes of many centuries is a road of innumerable wars, of cruelty and injustice, of sorrow and tears, of always hoping and always trying. Yet *Urzeit* and end-time are at the same time very close together: they meet in Jesus Christ, who stands in the center of the curse of the *Urzeit* — where Adam stood — and who, through death, has opened the road to paradise. His coming into the world ushers in the end-time, the new age, the new world. He gathers all things together again into the meaningful whole of God's eternal kingdom, and he infinitely transcends all human history. His death signifies the death of the human, of the *adam* in every human. His resurrection is new life. Those who are in Christ have broken the shackles of the *Urzeit,* and they partake of new life: they are "born into a living hope" in Christ Jesus. Behind all those long centuries of history lies another level, a much higher one: the reality of the cross. There our very humanity is transformed, there the curse is broken, and there paradise is reopened. Those who are in Christ Jesus have risen above history, are lifted up beyond the powers that make history what it is, and there they breathe the air of eternity: "The old is gone: see, everything has been made new."

The eternal meaning of the cross is expressed within the framework of history in the recurring celebration of the Lord's Supper. With each communion celebration, the cross is in direct contact with people as they live their lives in history. At that moment the tie with history is temporarily severed, and we humans are briefly in touch with those imperishable forces that tower over everything else. Time and eternity interlock; they are much closer to each other than we are aware of. History itself is merely a certain aspect of being in the world: it is not everything. In the proximity of the cross, all dates and places cease to have importance. We can say that Christ has been crucified in Jerusalem, but we can just as easily say that this happened in "Sodom and Egypt" (Rev. 11:18). We can just as

The Road to Life

easily maintain that he was killed by the chief priests and the scribes, or that he was killed by Herod and Pontius Pilate "together with the Gentiles and the people of Israel" (Acts 4:27), or by "the rulers of this age" (1 Cor. 2:8). The cross of Christ cannot be tied down to a single time and place: it is valid for all times and all people. Throughout the ages, the Lord's Supper depicts the eternal reality of the cross, in order that the people of all times and from every nation should gather at the foot of the cross.

There, at the cross, the attraction of the *Urzeit* ceases; complete silence reigns there. There the flaming sword is no longer a threat; there the Tree of the Knowledge of Good and Evil is no longer a temptation; there all the old memories sink away; there the complaint about the curse that came to rest on all of human life curse is silenced; there the old connection is shattered; and there the surety of being in Christ appears for us in all its beauty and glory. Death is no more there, nor mourning or tears, and all unacknowledged pain disappears there. All complaints about injustice and anguish are silenced there. Humans find themselves between the two paradises there, between the *Urzeit* and the end-time. The *Urzeit* sinks away from underneath their feet, and they reach out to the other age, the age in which our life and thoughts will be part of the vast community of the kingdom of God.

The Lord's Supper stands at the edge of history: it is the projection of the eternal into the framework of ordinary events. Every time we celebrate that sacrament, enormous vistas open up for us. Even though the world's happenings speed overhead, even though we are caught up in global conflicts and oppressions, the Lord's Supper conveys different values, and this makes us think of other grand designs. At the table of the Lord's Supper, I am reduced to being "human" in the fullest sense of the word: I become the *adam* who no longer is *adam* but who now is in Christ, with the Garden of Eden directly behind me and the new paradise just ahead of me. Both of them are within my grasp; I am in between them. But I am in Christ, and he is in me.

For a moment I shudder at the thought that I am included in the lightning flash of world history that speeds from *Urzeit* to end-time. But that feeling fades away, too, and I experience only that one overwhelming fact: "Our feet are standing in your gates, O Jerusalem" (Ps. 122:2). "When can I go and meet with God?" (Ps. 42:2). Gone is the long and terrible dream of sin, of the old connection, of the *adam* in me. I am beckoned by what is new in all its undiminished power. The veil before our face will be ripped away, the veil that "enfolds all peoples," the sheet that covers all nations. He will swallow up death forever. The sovereign Lord "will wipe away the tears from all faces" (Isa. 25:7-8). "If anyone hears my voice and opens the door, I will come in and eat with them, and they with me" (Rev. 3:20). "To him who overcomes, I will give the right to eat from the Tree of Life, which is in the paradise of God" (Rev. 2:7).

www.ingramcontent.com/pod-product-compliance
Lightning Source LLC
Chambersburg PA
CBHW031315150426
43191CB00005B/243